FAITH NEVER STANDS ALONE

How to Develop a Full Faith as a Bedrock for Life

Ronald W. Higdon

Energion Publications
Gonzalez, FL
2023

Copyright @ 2023, Ronald Higdon

Unless otherwise indicated, Scripture quotations are taken from the New Revised Standard Version, copyright 1989 by the Division of Christian Education & the National Council of the Churches of Christ.

Scripture quotations marked BARCLAY are taken from The New Testament by William Barclay, copyright 1999 by Westminster John Knox Press, Louisville.

Scripture quotations marked BARNSTONE are taken from The New Covenant by Willis Barnstone, copyright 2002 by The Berkley Publishing Group, New York.

Scripture quotations marked HART are taken from The New Testament by David Bentley Hart, copyright 2017 by Yale University Press, New Haven.

Scripture quotations marked HOLMAN are taken from Holman Christian Standard Bible, copyright 2004 by Holman Bible Publishers, Nashville.

Scripture quotations marked JB are taken from The Jerusalem Bible, copyright 1968 by Doubleday & Company, Garden City, New York.

Scripture quotations marked NEB are taken from The New English Bible, copyright 1961 by Oxford University Press, Cambridge.

Scripture quotations marked NEW are taken from A New New Testament edited by Hal Taussig, copyright 2013 by Houghton Mifflin Harcourt, Boston.

Scripture quotations marked NLT are taken from the Holy Bible, New Living Translation, copyright 1996, 2004, 2207, 2013 by Tyndale House Foundation. Used by permission of Tyndale House Publishers, Inc., Carol Stream, Illinois 60188. All rights reserved.

Scripture quotations marked PHILLIPS are taken from The New Testament in Modern English by J. B. Phillips, copyright 1968 by The Macmillan Company, New York.

Scripture quotations marked SCHONFIELD are taken from The Original New Testament by Hugh J. Schonfield, copyright 1998 by Element Books, Shaftesbury, Dorset.

Scripture quotations marked TNIV are taken from the Holy Bible, Today's New International Version, Copyright 2001, 2005 by International Bible Society. All rights reserved worldwide.

Scripture quotations marked WUEST are taken from The New Testament: An Expanded Translation by Kenneth S. Wuest, copyright 1961 by William B. Eerdmans Publishing Co., Grand Rapids.

Cover Design: Henry Neufeld
ISBN: 978-1-63199-843-0
eISBN: 978-1-63199-844-7
Library of Congress Control Number: 2022951966
Energion Publications — P.O. Box 841 — Gonzalez, FL 32560
(850) 525-3916 — Energion.com — pub@energion.com

Dedication

This book is dedicated to my wife of sixty-plus years, who has not only supported me in my ministry but has also made significant contributions. She read many of my sermons and manuscripts and made helpful and constructive observations about how they would come across to the reader or listener. It is with deep love and gratitude that I dedicate this book to Pat.

Table Of Contents

Preface vii
Introduction 1

1   Faith Is Not An Aladdin's Lamp 5
2   Cheap Faith Can Be Found On
    The Same Counter As Cheap Grace 13
3   Faith Is Always A Relational Matter 21
4   Faith Does Not Continue to Dance On The Foundation . 29
5   Faith Is A Kingdom Word 37
6   Faith Is Risky Business 47
7   Faith Always Involves Action 55
8   Faith and Perseverance Move In Lockstep 63
9   Faith and Courage Are Tightly Bound Together 71
10 Faith Does Not Protect Us
    from Life's Difficulties and Tragedies 79
11 Faith Always Comes In A Step Behind Love 87
12 Faith and Doubt Belong Together 95
13 Wrong Turns and Detours Are Part Of A Faith-Journey .. 105
14 What Kind Of Mountains Are Moved By Faith? 113
15 Faith Understands How to Ask Better Questions 123
16 Faith Has Nothing to Do With Perfection 133
17 Justice and Compassion Are Necessary for "Good Faith" 141
18 Faith Is A "Whatever" Stance 151

Conclusion:
    Faith Where I Am and How I Am
    Is The Place for Life and Meaning 159

    Bibliography Of Quoted Sources 161

Preface

The righteous live by their faith (Habakkuk 2:4).

"You Just Need More Faith."

How often have these words been spoken in all sincerity by someone who, intending to encourage us, now adds guilt to the negative emotions we already have? The meaning of the admonition: if you just had more faith everything would be okay. Many things are omitted from this simple instruction: What exactly is this faith you are talking about? Where do I go to get this faith? When will I ever get enough faith? If I have faith in sufficient quantity, will everything I ever need be taken care of? If I get the sufficiency of faith you are talking about will all my troubles be over? Will I be able to ask God for anything I feel I need and be assured of receiving it? Will all things be possible for me? Will faith be the magic key that unlocks all the blessings I am seeking? Will the necessary amount of faith put me more in control of what happens to me and those I love in this uncertain and threatening world?

When Talking About Faith, "Keep It Simple" Is Not Good Advice

Brevity, simplicity, and sentimentality are not helpful when talking about a subject as complex as faith (clarity is another matter). In too many recommendations and discussions I hear about faith, there is hardly any context and hardly any of the dimension and depth you will find in biblical faith. "Cheap faith" can be found on the same table as "cheap grace." Regardless of the markdown, they are not worth the price. If slogans of a bumper sticker faith are all that is necessary, Jesus would not have spent three years teaching his disciples what the life of faith is all about. He also promised additional lessons and insights that would be given them by the Holy Spirit (John 16:13).

Is Faith Equal to Belief?

Far too many associate faith with a set of beliefs. "My faith is solid; I know what I believe." Certainly, there is content to our faith, but this definition hardly touches the biblical approach to faith. When Jesus asked the struggling disciples, who feared their boat was about to sink, *"Where is your faith?"*, he was not asking for a recitation of creedal orthodoxy (Mark 4:35-41). Something far bigger was at stake. Even though Luther called James "a rather strawy epistle," it remains a part of the biblical canon. The author insists that faith is far more than believing there is a God: *You believe that God is one; you do well. Even the demons believe – and shudder* (James 2:29). His most shocking statements (the ones that probably gave Luther ulcers) are: *faith without works is dead* (2:17); *Do you want to be shown, you senseless person, that faith apart from works is barren?* (2:20); *For just as the body without the spirit is dead, so faith without works is also dead* (2:27).

Faith Is Never Solitary

The case for faith never standing alone, is clearly indicated in II Peter 1:5f:

You must make every effort to support your faith with goodness, and goodness with knowledge, and knowledge with self-control, and self-control with endurance, and endurance with godliness, and godliness with mutual affection, and mutual affection with love…Anyone who lacks these things is nearsighted and blind, and is forgetful of the cleansing of past sins.

The KJV of the above text begins with the words: *Add to your faith*. This list is certainly not meant to be comprehensive; it is only the beginning. "I've lost my faith," has been voiced by many good and sincere Christians who found that the onslaughts, disappointments, and tragedies of life did not respond to their faithful and on-going prayers. God let them down and they could not find in their own lives the confirmation of all the great promises of Scripture. God simply did not deliver, so what good had their faith done them?

How to Develop A Faith That Will Not Disappoint

> What did Jesus teach? He had no system, no summa, no code. God forbid! The only way to grasp his teaching is to read all the Gospels repeatedly, until its essence permeates the mind.[1]

I almost chose "How To Develop a Faith That Will Not Disappoint" as the subtitle for the book. It is my firm conviction that a faith of biblical depth and dimensions will not come up short. Exploring and talking about such a faith is challenging, demanding, and calls for the exploration of many of our favorite "cherry-picked" passages about the wonderful things faith delivers. What we will attempt to offer in this book is a faith firmly established on a solid rock that, unlike structures built on sand, will withstand the winds, floods, and storms of life that challenge and frustrate any faith that demands all the answers and the clarification of mystery, paradox, and ambiguity (Matthew 7:24-27). If you will stick with me, I believe we can discover together a faith that is amazing and achievable for all us ordinary folks. It promises what it can deliver: After all, *this is the victory that conquers (overcomes) the world - our faith* (I John 5:4).

---

1 Paul Johnson, *Jesus: A Biography From a Believer* (New York: Viking, 2010), 82.

Introduction

The Dimensions and Depths of Biblical Faith

If you check different translations, you will find some rendering the Greek word *pisteuo* as "believe" and some as "trust." One of the most important of these is found in John 14:1. Traditionally, the text has been read: "*Let not your heart be troubled: you believe in God believe also in me.*" In the context of this verse, which in John is part of Jesus' teaching in the Upper Room, the far better translation is: "*Do not let your hearts be troubled. Trust in God; trust also in me*" (TNIV). If you read chapters 13 through 17 (remember: there were no chapter or verse divisions in the original writing), trusting in God and trusting in Jesus, is the clear message.

Trust is always a relational word. It, like faith, never stands alone but always refers to trust in something or someone. Belief is certainly part of faith but, like the Pharisees, it is easy to allow what one believes to take priority over a relationship with God that provides the context for all one believes and practices. Jesus' Upper Room teaching implies from beginning to end that it rests solidly on a trusting relationship with the God who continues to manifest his trustworthiness. Another way of saying this is: we believe in a God who can be trusted.

The Hebrew word which lies at the base of the NT *pistis* and *pisteuein* is '*aman*'. Basically, this word means to be firm or solid, and hence to be true...to accept something as...firm, sure or true, trustworthy or dependable. [2]

The faith of the Gospels, like the OT faith, is not simply trust and confidence; it is trust and confidence which arise from faith, which in turn is an acceptance of a person and his claims.[3]

The earliest of the biblical stories raises a question that will continue throughout the pages of Scripture. It is raised by the one who will later be called "The Accuser" (HART). (David Bentley Hart translates "Satan" as "the Slanderer" in John 13:2 and as "the Accuser" in Luke 13:27). In discussing with Eve the limitations that God has placed on life in the Garden, the crafty question put to her is: "*Did God really say, 'You must not eat from any tree in the Garden'?*" (Genesis 3:1). The response given is that God permits any tree's fruit to be eaten except for the tree in the middle of the garden, "*the Tree of the Knowing of Good and Evil.*"[4]

NO TRUST: HIDING IN FEAR

The Accuser's attack on God can be simply stated: "You can't trust God! He's holding out on you. The day you eat that forbidden fruit you will be like him. You will know what he knows! Trust me! Just take a bite!" The next scene finds God "*walking in the garden in the cool of the day*" and calling out, "*Where are you?*" (3:8). The response God receives is (my paraphrase): "We are hiding because we are afraid." Later we will discuss a basic premise: the opposite of faith is not doubt, but fear. Fear is a term of separation in which the relationship of trust has been broken. The remainder of the Bible makes the case for God's trustworthiness and the futility of living in fear. The accounts of the Incarnation in Matthew

---

2   John L. McKenzie, *Dictionary of the Bible* (New York: Macmillan Publishing Company, 1965), 267.
3   Ibid, 268.
4   Everett Fox, *The Five Books of Moses* (New York: Shocken Books, 1995), 20.

Faith Never Stands Alone

and Luke contain a surprising number of "fear nots." Surprising until you realize just how much they continue to be needed.

As we move through the following chapters, we will find that even our orthodoxy rests on the foundation of belief as trust in the God who continually reminds us of his love and faithfulness. Along the way, we will continue to encounter in various disguises the voice of the Accuser asking, "Are you sure you can really trust God? He may be holding out on you. He may not really want what is best for you after all." Well, let's just see about that.

The journey we will take through the pages that follow:

1. Faith is not a talisman.
2. Cheap faith and cheap grace can be found at the same "Bargain Religion" stores.
3. Faith is always a matter of personal pronouns.
4. The basics of faith are meant to be built on.
5. The Sermon on the Mount is the description of Kingdom people.
6. Faith is not for those who want to play it safe.
7. Faith is a verb.
8. Faith isn't a quitter.
9. Frequently, you can hardly tell the difference between faith and courage.
10. Faith acknowledges the incomprehensibility of evil.
11. Without love, there is nothing left.
12. Faith must always have "negative capability."
13. Faith does not provide a GPS.
14. "So much more" is the watchword of faith.
15. Faith communities should be safe places for all our questions.
16. Nobody has their act all together.
17. Faith is willing to listen to the voices of the powerless.
18. There is a lot of acceptance and surrender in faith.

Conclusion: Spirituality is about honoring the human journey.

Each chapter contains five sections: Biblical Perspectives; Exploring and Considering; Quotes Worth Thinking About;

Coming to Some Conclusions; and Questions for Reflection and Conversation.

It is my firm conviction that faith should touch all areas of our lives and "whole faith" is the term I use to describe the completeness, the wholeness, the fullness that God intends for our lives. Faith is never meant to be an addendum that shores us up when we are about to go under. It is meant to be the solid rock-foundation on which our lives are built (see Matthew 7:24-27). You might feel that some of the things discussed in these pages don't have much to do with faith. I'll try to make the case that they do because they have to do with our living and functioning at our best as human beings created in the image of God.

A bibliography of quoted sources will be found on page 161 and following. Books cited do not necessarily imply agreement or endorsement.

I

Faith Is Not An Aladdin's Lamp

Biblical Perspectives

Taken out of context (which includes the totality of the biblical witness), there are verses that appear to promise such a magic lamp. In the well-known story, Aladdin has but to rub the lamp, the genie appears, and whatever he wishes is brought about by the captive magician in the bottle. Here are a couple of the texts that appear to tell us God will do whatever we ask if we only have enough faith:

> *Afterward, the disciples asked Jesus privately, "Why couldn't we cast out that demon?"*
> *"You didn't have enough faith," Jesus told them. "I assure you, even if you had faith as small as a mustard seed you could say to this mountain, 'Move from here to there,' and it would move. Nothing would be impossible"* (Matthew 17:19-20).
>
> *Are any among you sick? They should call for the elders of the church and have them pray over them, anointing them with oil in the name of the Lord. And their prayer offered in faith will heal the sick and the Lord will make them well. And anyone who has committed sins will be forgiven* (James 5:14-15).

One of life's discoveries is that too many mountains have not been moved and too many people have not been healed – even after bushels of mustard seeds. Faith is not magic that calls God into our service and automatically brings our wishes and prayers to fruition. We are not in charge and God is not captive even to our prayers. He is not the Divine Bellhop who is always on call to be of service. Faith is not an Aladdin's lamp.

If the verses from Matthew and James were literally true in all circumstances, it would put us in the driver's seat of our lives. We would determine what was needed, what was best for our lives, and what God needed to do. (Many times, in my life, what I really wanted and felt to be best for me, I later discovered would have been just the opposite. My future vision is far from 20/20.) We are seeking to answer the basic question that surfaced in Eden, "Who's in charge here, anyway?" The Accuser told Adam and Eve they were. In our weaker moments, it continues to be the lie whispered in our ears.

Even the Ark of the Covenant couldn't force God's hand

Following the failure of the military mission to defeat the Philistines, the consensus became clear. They needed to do something to ensure that God was with them. The Ark was the most sacred item in their possession; it was where the presence of God was most clearly focused. The decision to carry it into battle was the guarantee that God would grant victory over their enemy. His very Name would be at stake; he could not possibly allow another deity to defeat his people.

This time - "So let it be written, so let it be done" - didn't happen for the Hebrews. They lost the battle and the Ark was captured and carried away into captivity (1 Samuel chapter 4). This simply was not possible. (The same attitude prevails later about the inviolability of Jerusalem and the Temple.) The Ark was not the talisman it had seemed. It did not guarantee either the presence of God or victory. My contention: the people had forgotten that it was the Ark "of the Covenant." Its purpose (and power) lay in their relationship of commitment to the God whose commitment to them it symbolized. Isolated from that relationship, it represented no more than a "lucky" rabbit's foot (which many have observed proved none too lucky for the rabbit).

Faith is not something "out there." It is not something separate from us. In Raiders of the Lost Ark, one of the Nazi officers tells the others that it is nothing less than a "transmitter for talking to God." No. That is the mistake the Hebrews made: they thought it was God's private, direct line. Connection and results were guaranteed because they were built into the Ark itself. There is nothing about faith that coincides with this mechanistic approach.

Exploring and Considering

Several years ago, a sensation was created by the discovery of the prayer of Jabez (which had been in 1 Chronicles 4:10 for centuries). A book based on the text and prayer was inappropriately titled: "*The Prayer of Jabez: Breaking Through to the Blessed Life.*"[5] In case you have forgotten (and most people had previously taken little notice), the text reads:

> *Jabez called on the God of Israel saying, "Oh that you would bless me and enlarge my border, and that your hand might be with me, and that you would keep me from hurt and harm!" And God granted what he asked* (1 Chronicles 4:10).

For this Jabez lamp, the calling forth of the "genie" seems simple, straightforward, and guarantees affirmative answers. As is so often the case, a little bit of exegesis changes the picture considerably. Jabez is "a name introduced abruptly into a list of descendants of Judah…"[6] *He is distinguished; honored more than his brothers; more distinguished than any of his brothers* (NLT); or *ranked higher than his brothers* (NEB). We are given no additional information

---

5   Bruce Wilkinson, *The Prayer of Jabez* (Sisters, OR: Multnomah Publishers, 2000).
6   *The Interpreter's Dictionary of the Bible,* Vol 2 (New York: Abingdon Press, 1962), 779.

about his life or his contributions except for the brief prayer for blessings and protection. The only other addition is supplied by his mother: *his mother named him Jabez, saying, "Because I bore him in pain"* (4:9). Not much on which to base the foundation for a way to get God to answer your prayers.

Basing "How to Receive God's Promises" on a single verse of Scripture containing the prayer of an individual mentioned nowhere else in the Bible, appears at first glance to be the epitome of "proof-texting." It also ignores what I contend is the basic principle of interpreting any verse of Scripture: the totality of the biblical witness (this idea will keep coming up because it is so readily ignored). There is a plethora of material on prayer in the Bible, including many cries from the psalmists about God's lack of responding to pleas for assistance and rescue. And not to be put in a secondary place, there is Jesus' response when the disciples ask, "Teach us to pray, as John taught his disciples" (Luke 11:1). Jesus gives what is commonly called "The Lord's Prayer," but which more accurately should be labeled "The Disciples' Prayer" or "The Model Prayer." In Matthew 6:9-13, the model prayer concludes some explicit instructions on how our praying should be done.

Unfortunately, I put the book on the prayer of Jabez on the same table where you can find copies of cheap faith and cheap grace (more about these in chapter two). Here is an actual review about the book placed on Amazon:

> Great book. I honestly started praying the prayer and within a month I was able to acquire 4 rental properties with less than $500 of my own money. I had previously owned 0 properties. Talk about a literal expansion of territory. The key is to use this prayer in its FULLNESS as I did and I noticed almost instant results that were otherwise unexplainable.
>
> There is something about the peace of mind that this prayer provides and a deeper connection to Your God, whomever that may be.

The emphasis of this testimony (and, evidently the praying done) was the kind of spirituality that keeps us in the center of everything. Jesus' model prayer begins with the emphasis on the Father whose name (Yahweh) is kept holy and sacred. The first request in his prayer gives the direction of the entire prayer: *Thy kingdom come and thy will be done.* Reading the Sermon on the Mount (Matthew 5 – 7) gives a pretty clear picture of how this kind of emphasis will shape our praying. There are indeed blessings to be had (as the Beatitudes clearly spell out) but most of these blessings are recognized only by those whose direction is Kingdom living (more about this later).

Quotes Worth Thinking About

> So my advice is this – don't look for proofs. Don't' bother with them at all. They are never sufficient to the question, and they're always a little impertinent, I think, because they claim for God a place within our intellectual grasp.[7]
>
> The Lord absolutely transcends any understanding I have of Him, which makes loyalty to Him a different thing from loyalty to whatever customs and doctrines and memories I happen to associate with Him.[8]

One of my favorite lines (and scenes) in *The Wizard of Oz* is: "Pay no attention to the man behind the curtain." Of course, that's where the attention needs to be focused because it is the source of all the wizardry (thunder, smoke, booming voice, etc.). When our heroes look behind the curtain everything changes in their relationship to the "Wizard." In pagan temples, if you looked behind the sacred curtain you would find some kind of image of the god being worshipped. The Temple in Jerusalem was unique. If you could look behind the curtain that separated the Holy Place from the Holy of Holies what you found was – nothing! No image could capture Yahweh who refused to be imprisoned in any human shaping or evaluation. The revelation of his name to Moses was indicative of the inability to define him in any way. Moses wanted

---

7 Marilynne Robinson, *Gilead* (London: Vigero Press, 2020), 204.
8 Ibid., 268-269.

to know how to respond when the Israelites asked who had sent him. *You shall say to the Israelites, "I AM has sent me to you... YHWH (Yahweh), the God of your ancestors, the God of Abraham, the God of Isaac, and the God of Jacob, has sent me to you: This is my name forever..."* (Exodus 3:14-15, HOLMAN). Even the most orthodox theologians – for example, Thomas Aquinas – emphasize the incomprehensibility of God as an essential count to anthropomorphic conceptions.[9]

COMING TO SOME CONCLUSIONS

> *Pistis* is too often translated as "faith" or "belief." *Pistis*, and its Latin equivalent fides, in antiquity connoted "steadfastness" or "conviction" or "loyalty."[10]
>
> Faith in America as it exists and how it is practiced in the heartland is more about control than it is about freedom.[11]

Ancient pagan worship and sacrifices were all about getting the attention of the gods and persuading them to do something. Offerings were meant to placate and win favor. They were a way to control their gods. The biblical teaching is that we already have God's favor. We already have God's attention (just read the Psalms). We already are assured of God's presence. Our faith (among other things) involves steadfastness, conviction, and loyalty. God is not a quiz show host waiting for us to say the secret word (Groucho Marx, *You Bet Your Life*) in order to give you the prize. We don't need a magic lamp or even magic prayers. We are already in God's "blessing plan" and what we are called to do is to align ourselves with God's purposes and plans for our lives in order that we might receive those blessings and be those blessings to those around us.

---

9 Gary Gutting, *What Philosophy Can Do* (New York: W.W. Norton, 2015), 126.
10 Paula Fredriksen, *Paul: The Pagan's Apostle* (New Haven: Yale University Press, 2017), 119-120.
11 Lyn Lenz, *God Land* (Bloomington: Indiana University Press, 2019), 133.

QUESTIONS FOR REFLECTION AND CONVERSATION

1. How do you deal with your unanswered prayers?
2. How would you define your faith?
3. Do you agree that the prayer of Jabez falls short of a complete theology of prayer?

2

Cheap Faith Can Be Found On The Same Counter As Cheap Grace

Biblical Perspectives

Some context for this section

"Cheap grace and costly grace" was a phrase which soon spread far beyond specialist theological circles. It appeared first in The Cost of Discipleship (by Dietrich Bonhoeffer), the first drafts of which go back to 1931-32 and which was published in 1937. The formula arose from his reading of Kierkegaard.[12]

Bonhoeffer defined cheap grace as the following: The grace which amounts to justification of sin with the justification of the repentant sinner who departs from sin and from whom sin departs. Cheap grace is not the kind of forgiveness of sin which frees us from the toils of sin. Cheap grace is the grace we bestow on ourselves...Cheap grace is the preaching of forgiveness without requiring repentance, baptism without church discipline, communion without confession, absolution without personal confession. Cheap grace is grace without dis-

---

12 Eberhard Bethge, *Costly Grace* (San Francisco: Harper & Row, 1979), 150.

cipleship, grace without the cross, grace without Jesus, living and incarnate.[13]

One of my favorite cartoons has a scene of misty clouds with three people in line before someone behind a podium, looking into an open book. Behind him is a huge closed gate. To the left is an open gate through which a man is flying like superman. The open gate is marked "E-Z Pass."[14] The artist, Bob Mankoff, cartoon editor of The New Yorker, has provided without words the perfect picture of cheap grace: grace without demands, a grace with no strings attached. In other words, grace without any biblical context.

Is there an E-Z Pass gate of grace? Bonhoeffer insisted there was not. Writing during the time of Hitler's rise to power in Germany, his voice spoke of both the theological and political dimensions of life. Shortly before the end of WWII, it cost him his life. For him, the cost of discipleship was the supreme cost. For me, the best summary of Bonhoeffer's thought is this line: "Cheap grace is the grace we bestow on ourselves." The focus of grace is shifted from God to us. Its shape and contours are formed by what we believe best suits our personal needs and how we perceive religious matters ought to work. It is all about personal spirituality and not about "belonging" to something larger than ourselves. It is echoed in the often-heard testimony: "I'm not religious; I'm spiritual."

What immediately comes to mind is what I believe to be a dangerous translation (misinterpretation) of Scripture. Michael Shermer[15] translates Luke7:20-21: *And when he was demanded of the Pharisees, when the kingdom of God should come, he answered them and said, "The kingdom of God cometh not with observation: Neither shall they say, Lo here! Or, lo there! for the kingdom of God is within you."* Some have concluded that God is not "out there" but God

---

13   Michael Van Dyke, *The Story of Dietrich Bonhoeffer* (Uhrichsville, OH: Barbour Publishing, 2001), 110-111.
14   Bob Mankoff, *How About Never – Is Never Good for You?* (New York: Henry Holt, 2014), 27.
15   Michael Shermer, *Heaven on Earth* (New York: St. Martin's Griffin, 2018), 66.

Faith Never Stands Alone

is "in me." A god of my own choosing, a god of my own making. The better and more accurate translation is *"behold the kingdom of God is among you" (or in your midst)*. In this context, Jesus is referring to himself, the one who is standing before them. Here is the difference between a Christ-centered kingdom and an individual, personal-centered kingdom (of my choosing and making).

One of my favorite gospel stories is about the disciples being caught in a life-threatening storm while crossing the Sea of Galilee (Mark 4:35-41). This body of water is subject to sudden and violent storms. (I witnessed one on a visit to Israel that was frightening to behold even from the shore.) With Jesus asleep on a cushion in the stern of the boat, here is the literal translation of what was happening: *A great storm came, and the waves kept dashing into the boat, so that the boat was actually filling* (NEW). Even experienced fishermen feared for their lives in the unanimous cry: *"Teacher, do you not care that we are perishing?"*

Jesus gets up and "rebukes" the wind and the sea (the same word is used when he rebukes evil spirits); the wind ceases and there is a great calm. Then Jesus asks what might be considered an unnecessary and even inconsiderate question: *"Why are you afraid? Have you still no faith?"* The rebuke given in the same story in Luke 8:22 is *"Where is your confidence?"* (NEW). My response would have been: "To tell you the truth, it got drenched!" The big question: What kind of faith, what kind of confidence did the disciples have that it could be shattered by a storm? Jesus had asked to be taken to the other side of the lake. Didn't that ensure a calm sea? They never expected this kind of danger with Jesus on board.

It may seem a harsh judgment but I believe the disciples on this occasion illustrated what is meant by cheap faith. It was a "sunshine" and "fair-weather" faith that was unprepared for the inclement weather of life. Rachel Held Evans speaks to that kind of fair-weather faith in this line: "Church books are written by people with a plan and ten steps, not by Christians just hanging on by their fingernails."[16] With Jesus in the boat, the disciples must have felt they had an insurance policy that guaranteed a safe crossing. Their faith had no place for high winds and a boat filling with water.

Exploring and Considering

> The writer of Hebrews is not talking about faith as that "sunny-side-of-the-street" optimism that borders on baptized superstition and that is so prevalent in popular theology. Rather, he is talking about faith as trust despite the darkness, faith as believing that it is God's unfailing nature to birth unanticipated goodness out of inexplicable difficulty and unbearable pain.[17]

"Faith as trust despite the darkness" describes the times in which faith is most needed, when the sunny-side-of-the-street is not available. When "inexplicable difficulty and unbearable pain" are rejected as not being possible in the life of those who are "truly faithful" (whatever that means), it is nothing less than the rejection of the reality of living in a world that is not yet fully redeemed (Romans 8:19-23). Richard Rohr, one of my favorite writers, describes our authentic hope and our daily predicaments:

> The contemplative mind got in the way of our left-brain philosophy of progress, science, and development, which were very good and necessary in their own way – but not for soul knowledge. What we lost was almost any notion of paradox, mystery, or the wisdom of unknowing and unsayability – which are the open-ended qualities that make biblical faith so dynamic, creative, and nonviolent.[18]

Cheap faith almost always lacks "any notion of paradox, mystery, or the wisdom of unknowing and unsayability." It usually

---

16 Rachel Held Evans, *Searching for Sunday* (Nashville: Nelson Books, 2015), xvi.
17 Charles E. Poole, *Beyond the Broken Lights* (Macon: Smyth & Helwys, 2000), 37.
18 Richard Rohr, *The Universal Christ* (New York: Convergent, 2019), 210.

supplies slogans, selected texts, and philosophies to "explain" or "de-mystify" situations when all the lights go out. There is little concept of the wisdom of unknowing and unsayability. Job's three friends are perfect examples of those who are at their best in the compassion of silent presence but at their worst in attempts to unravel the mystery of unbelievable suffering. In the end, God announces that the friends got it all wrong and Job in his unknowing and unsayability got it right.

The Scriptures are filled with people who struggled with difficulties and tragedies that made no sense and certainly bore no relationship to the godly lives they were attempting to live. When Gideon received the greeting from a divine messenger, "*The Lord is with you, you mighty warrior*," the response appears both appropriate and shocking, "*If the Lord is with us, why then has all this happened to us?*" (Judges 6:12-13). The Midianite oppression was so severe that Gideon had to "*beat out wheat in the wine press, to hide it from (them)*" (6:11). Fear and privation ruled the day; the hand of the Lord was nowhere to be seen. Trust in God was not "paying off." Things were not working as they were supposed to. "Why" remains the major question voiced by the people of God when inexplicable difficulty and unbearable pain come to call. Although in this instance, God had sent a prophet to announce that reverence to the Amorite gods on the part of some was a breach of their covenant with him (Judges 6:10). It is evident Gideon had not gotten this message – note that it is not delivered to him by the angel. The message he does get is the call to action; he is to drive the Midianites from the land. Later, we'll talk about the role of action in faith.

Quotes Worth Thinking About

> But if the world is watching, we might as well tell the truth. And the truth is, the church doesn't offer a cure. It doesn't offer a quick fix. The church offers death and resurrection. The church offers the messy, inconvenient, gut-wrenching,

never-ending work of healing and reconciliation. The church offers grace. Anything else we try to peddle is snake oil. It's not the real thing.[19]

Rachel Held Evans is certainly not peddling snake oil! She always seems to have a shocking, but redemptive, word to offer when a good dose of reality is called for. When your personal life, as well as the lives of those around you, is filled with sufficient pain and suffering, you soon become aware there are no cheap solutions. The cross is testimony to the costly answer God found necessary; a cheap solution was not available. To Jesus' plea, *"If it be possible, remove this cup from me"* (Mark 14:36), the evident answer must have been that God had no other plan. His way of redemption involved a cross. Many might ask, "Were things really that bad?" The testimony of Scripture and of life is: yes, they were – and are!

> Having a slight intellectual grasp of a concept and thinking you've got it is a fatal spiritual flaw, one that's infected the New Age movement and led to egotism and attitudes of spiritual superiority.[20]

When anyone asks me where I am in my Christian pilgrimage, I always reply, "I'm just a beginner." This is not only a stance of humility but of actuality. I continue to realize how much there is yet to be explored, understood, and put into practice. "Under Construction" still remains my favorite T-shirt slogan. The most frequent title given to Jesus in the Gospels is "Teacher." It seems to be so appropriate that one translation changes *"disciples"* to *"students"* (BARNSTONE, Mark 3:7; 8:4). And, as I observed in another book, nowhere does Jesus pass out graduation certificates. School is never out and the lessons are never over. Which brings me to the last quote in this section.

> Peanuts as a touchstone and balm in tough times: Unlike so many other venerated objects in U.S. pop culture, it was sweet without being stupid, reassuring without being infantile.

---

19 Rachel Held Evans, *Searching for Sunday,* 209.
20 Pedram Shojai, *The Art of Stopping* (New York: Rodale, 2017), 180.

In the dark era in which it began, it served much the same function as I Love Lucy. The difference was it had brains.[21]

You have heard many times but it bears repeating: Many have called this the information age; no one has called it the age of wisdom. One thing stands out with the characters in Peanuts: "They live like kids, but think like philosophers."[22]

That is why I understand Chris Ware in his observation: "As I've said elsewhere, Charles Schultz is the only author whom I've been reading my entire life."[23] I continue to use the "wisdom" of the Peanuts' gang to pepper my workshops; they usually bring a smile and an accompanying, "Oh, yes!"

Coming to Some Conclusions

Cheap faith is not so much bad faith as it is faith that promises too much for too little effort and participation on our part. It lacks the things the following chapters in this book contend are all a part of developing a full faith as a bed rock for life. "Cheap faith" cannot stand the challenges and tests that come. I have heard many sermons on how God tests our faith. My contention is that it is life that tests our faith. James 1:13 – *No one, when tempted, should say, "I am being tempted by God"; for God cannot be tempted by evil and he himself tempts no one."* I believe the word "tested" can easily be substituted for the word "tempted."

This quote, I'm certain, will not find full agreement, but I include it for the same reason that Jesus used parables: "To remind, provoke, refine, confront, and disturb."[24]

> Even though properly basic beliefs about such matters (religion, ethics, politics, etc.) do not require prior philosoph-

---

21 Andrew Blauner, ed., *The Peanuts Papers* (New York: Library of America, 2019), 46.
22 Ibid, 67.
23 Ibid, 96.
24 Rachel Held Evans, *Inspired* (New York: Nelson Books, 2018), 161.

ical justification, they do need intellectual maintenance, which typically involves philosophical thinking.[25]

From early on, Christian intellectuals employed ideas from pagan Greek philosophers to clarify, develop, and defend their convictions – the enterprise of (Anselm's) "faith seeking understanding" (their version of intellectual maintenance).[26]

Lest some fear this is all a secular pursuit, we need to remember that Anselm (1033-1109) was a monk, theologian, and Archbishop of Canterbury. These early church fathers were all concerned about searching for a deeper understanding of faith that rested in the life, ministry, death, and resurrection of Jesus Christ. Earlier, Augustine of Hippo (354-430) used a similar phrase: "Believe that you may understand."

Perhaps the subtitle of this book could have been: "Faith Seeking Understanding."

QUESTIONS FOR REFLECTION AND CONVERSATION

1. Does your faith make room for mystery, paradox, and ambiguity?
2. How do you respond to the phrase, "Faith as trust despite the darkness"?
3. What does the translation of "disciples" as "students" say to you?

---

25   Gary Gutting, *What Philosophy Can Do*, 247.
26   Ibid, 252.

3

FAITH IS ALWAYS A RELATIONAL MATTER

BIBLICAL PERSPECTIVES

Sometimes (we) are urged to trust in the Word of God (Psalms 119:43), but more usually it is faith in God himself that is sought. *Trust in the Lord with all your heart, and do not rely on your own insight* (Proverbs 3:5). Trust in idols is often denounced (Isaiah 42:17; Habakkuk 2:18).[27]

The well-meaning spoken word of encouragement, "Have faith!", should always include this question on the part of the receiver: "Have faith in what?" Having faith in faith is so much like whistling in the dark or hoping against hope. Faith is not some nebulous something that is out there waiting for us to grab on. Faith without a source, a reason, a place to stand, is faith grounded in nothing except itself. Marva Dawn is correct: biblical faith is almost always directed to God.

Frequent polls are taken to ascertain how many people believe in God (or a god).

There is a profound difference between believing in a personal God and knowing God personally, that is, relating to

---

27 Marva Dawn, *In the Beginning God* (Downers Grove, IL: InterVarsity Press, 2009), 496.

Reality intimately. Believing in a personal God – giving ascent to a supernatural entity with a personality – may or may not make a difference in the life of the believer. When belief does not richly transform one's experience, such belief becomes a booby prize. In contrast, when we relate to Reality personally – knowing that each of us is accepted just as we are, and trusting that it's possible to interpret everything real in one's life as a gift and a blessing in disguise; this will always transform any of us.[28]

Big sidebar: before too many jump to false conclusions over the title of the book, *Thank God for Evolution,* from which the above quote comes, I ask the important question: Have you read the book? When you read it, you discover a Christian minister's attempt to reconcile science and religion that has won praise from both the religious and scientific circles. You don't have to agree with all the author's conclusions to find your life enriched and blessed – and better informed – about both science and faith.

James 2:19 is the classic rebuttal to the proposition that all you have to do is believe there is a God: *You believe that God is one; you do well. Even the demons believe – and shudder.* The author of James is arguing that faith divorced from works is empty. It also shows that faith divorced from relationship to God is empty. And by relationship, I'm not suggesting it is necessary to have a burning bush or Damascus Road experience. For most of us, our relationship to God is found in quiet, devotional, contemplative moments.

> No matter what other suggestions scholars make about the meaning of being "in the image," they all agree that it includes being in relationship.[29]

At the very least, this relationship involves what Mark's Gospel tells us about Jesus' relationship with the Father: *In the morning, while it was still very early, (Jesus) got up and went out to a deserted place, and there he prayed* (Mark 1:35). Prayer is basically a conversation with God. It is a connecting of our spirits with his Spirit

---

28 Michael Dodd, *Thank God for Evolution* (San Francisco: Council Oak Books, 2007), 112-113.
29 Marva Dawn, *In the Beginning God,* 42.

in the attempt to establish communication which is only possible because the Psalms (Israel's hymn book and prayer book) are full of promises that God listens to us when we pray. Faith begins with the assurance that our relationship with God assures us that space will be provided for our voice and guidance will be given. This is just another one of the amazing grace-provisions that fills the Scriptures.

Exploring And Considering

> We might honor the Jewish custom by using the unpronounceable four letter (called "the tetragragrammaton") YHWH. That way, we will always pause at the word and praise God's covenant faithfulness.
> This is the Promise Keeper, whose steadfast love and faithfulness would unceasingly be with them/us![30].

The utterly unique aspect of the God of Israel was that he was a covenant-making God. He did not wait for sacrifices or offerings to get his attention or stir him to action. He initiated pledges of his presence and his aid based solely on his steadfast love and faithfulness. Granted, there needed to be reciprocal allegiance on the part of the people, but even with their continued covenant-breaking behavior, God kept reaching out and opening the door to covenant-renewal. This covenant making and promise keeping God took it to its highest level in the Upper Room when Jesus said, "*This cup is the covenant in my blood.*" All past promises, covenants, and "yeses" from God now reach their fulfillment and completion in the giving of his Son on the cross. God will do whatever it takes to reconcile us to himself. God will do whatever it takes to mend the fractured relationship with his creation. God will do whatever it takes to bring us back to himself.

> I am in the camp of those who cheer the knocking down of gates and walls around the sacraments, especially the place called "The Lord's Table," "The Lord's Supper," The Mass, the

---
30 Ibid, 69.

Eucharist, or Holy Communion. When Christians of various communions recognize and invite each other to this central mystery and observance, "oneness" becomes visible and tangible as they participate."[31]

When we say that faith is always a relational matter, we mean not only a relationship to God but a relationship to other people. Gathering around "The Lord's Table" brings us to the central mystery of redemption, mercy, and grace of the God who wants to be with us – and who wills for us to be with one another with that same kind of love, mercy, and grace. Many have observed that, biblically, there is no such thing as a solitary Christian. What is so disturbing about today's emphasis on spirituality without religion, is that it usually means spirituality without participation in a community. Hebrews 10:24-25 is the great reminder: *And let us consider how we may spur one another on toward love and good deeds, not giving up meeting together, as some are in the habit of doing, but encouraging one another…*(TNIV).

I know from over sixty years of experience, the challenges of living and working in the community of the saints (Paul's designation for all Christians), but I also know the blessings, which far outnumber the difficulties. I do not need to tell you that all relationships can be bumpy at times due to the very fact that human beings are involved. Even Paul and Barnabas had a major conflict involving John Mark that eventually led to separation (Acts 15:36-41). But, when the goals are love, good deeds, and encouragement, the ride is worth the jolts that come along the way. These words remain true: "Blest be the tie that binds our hearts in Christian love. The fellowship of kindred minds is like to that above."

> "The Christian life…is ultimately not about believing or about being good. Rather…it is about a relationship with God that involves us on a journey of transformation." Marcus Borg.[32]

---

31 Martin E. Marty, *When Faiths Collide*, 110.
32 Tom Stell, *A Faith Worth Believing* (New York: HarperSanFrancisco, 2004), 157.

I have many disagreements with Marcus Borg, but he is right on target – with one exception. I would modify his statement to read: "The Christian life is ultimately about a relationship with God and other people that involves us on a journey of transformation." God's people have been instrumental in so much of the transformation that has taken place in my life. Those who have been a major influence in my life comprise a list so long I can hardly believe it myself.

> A mark of lifelong learners is recognizing that they can learn something from everyone they meet.
> Arrogance leaves us blind to our weaknesses. Humility is a reflective lens: it helps us see them clearly. Confident humility is a corrective lens: it enables us to overcome those weaknesses.[33]

When I was a seminary student and pastoring a rural church, I had a couple of people who commented that I probably didn't have to work too hard on my sermons because I was in a country church. I quickly corrected that misconception. The two rural churches I was privileged to pastor contained some of the most committed and knowledgeable people I have ever known. Several were some of the best Sunday School teachers I have ever encountered in any church, anywhere. I learned a great deal from people who were "of the land" but also shared a wealth of wisdom on living as Christians in today's world. Many of them knew far more than I did and I believe I did develop confident humility that enabled me to see some of my weaknesses and, with their help, to begin to overcome them.

QUOTES WORTH THINKING ABOUT

> In a 1982 public television documentary, Updike's son David reproached his father, who, "decided at an early age that his writing had to take precedence over his relations with real people." Updike acknowledged the charge: "my duty as a

---

33 Adam Grant, *Think Again* (New York: Viking, 2021), 54.

writer…takes precedence for me over all these other considerations."³⁴

Far too many of us, at one time or another, have allowed our work to take precedence over everything else, but I don't believe any have done it with the dogged intentionality of John Updike. His duty as a writer appears to have blotted out all other duties – especially those of father and husband. He won the Pulitzer Prize for Fiction more than once but no awards were ever presented by his family. I often wonder how his life would have been different, if his honors would have been any less, if he had considered his role in the human family and the value of relationship to his personal and emotional life. Just a question for pondering.

> One afternoon in Maryland in 1983, Daryl Davis arrived at a lounge to place the piano at a country music gig. It wasn't his first time being the only Black man in the room. Before the night was out, it would be his first time having a conversation with a white supremacist…
>
> Soon the man was admitting that he'd never had a drink with a Black person before. Eventually he explained to Daryl why. He was a member of the Ku Klux Klan….
>
> Daryl burst out laughing…
>
> It was the first time he remembers facing overt racism, and although he could justifiably have gotten angry, he was bewildered: "How can you hate me when you don't even know me?"³⁵

I am immediately reminded of the exchange early in the Jurassic Park movie between the owner of the park and a person he is attempting to persuade to visit the park and provide an endorsement. The owner laments the difficulties he is encountering because of lawyers who see too many potential dangers in the facility. He finally asks, "I just hate lawyers, don't you?" There is a period of hesitation until the reply comes: "Well, I really don't know any."

---

34 Peter C. Brown, *Listening for God* (Macon: Mercer University Press, 2020), 108.
35 Adam Grant, *Think Again*, 121-122.

Stereotypes based on race, occupation, or any other part of a person's life should never be a basis for judgment. "All _____" (fill in the blank) cannot be labeled with the same sticker. Until you know someone individually (personally) you do not know them. When Daryl asked the KKK member how he could hate him when he didn't even know him, we are not given the reply. What we do know is that a friendship developed and the man ended up leaving the KKK. In this case, knowing one Black man changed his perception of an entire race (or at least made him recognize the necessity of avoiding blanket judgments). Knowing one lawyer can/should have the same effect.

Martin E. Marty, in *When Faiths Collide*, addresses the same issue in the religious world. I believe his suggestion (advice) applies to making all relationships healthier and stronger.

> The favorite term for this time was dialogue. More recently the term and concept of conversation parallels or replaces dialogue, which assumes a somewhat more formal discourse…Conversation…is moved by the questions, and takes on something of the character of an inconclusive game. One does not hear claims such as "I won that conversation!" And conversation is especially appealing because it invites in on equal terms host and guest, belonger and stranger, the committed and the less committed, the informed and the less informed. Across boundaries of faiths they have no referee or determiner of a winner….[36].

So, how about a conversation?

COMING TO SOME CONCLUSIONS

"People who need people are the luckiest people in the world." I remember when these words began a popular song that was used in many workshops. The urge and necessity of relating to others begins as soon as we are old enough to recognize that there are others. In penal institutions, the most severe punishment is solitary

---

36   Martin E. Marty, *When Faiths Collide*, 91.

confinement. During this current Pandemic, isolation has crippled many who have escaped the disease. At the moment (March of 2021), Florida is hosting massive Spring Breaks of those who are pushing the envelope because they simply cannot live any longer without interacting with their peers. Our prayer is that another COVID- 19 surge will not be the result.

Many have written that the desire for relationships is imprinted in our DNA; one of the basic meanings of being created in the image of God is that we are made to be in relationship – with God and with other human beings. Most biblical scholars are convinced that the very concept of the Trinity (Father, Son, and Holy Spirit) indicates that God has always been a God in relationship – even before the creation of the world. (More about the Trinity in a future chapter.)

Faith is not a transaction in which we get a ticket to future eternal life. It is a seat at the Father's table where there is joy, laughter, and the establishment of on-going relationships that enrich and nourish our lives. And it provides our introduction to the diversity of those who make up Kingdom citizens.

> For Augustine, it is not so much that we discover God in ourselves as that we find ourselves in God. We are *in* God *with* others.[37]

QUESTIONS FOR REFLECTION AND DISCUSSION

1. Why should we remember that God is a covenant-making God?
2. Have you learned things from some "unlikely" people?
3. How did the story of Daryl Davis speak to you?

---

37 David Tracy, *Filaments* (Chicago: University of Chicago Press, 2020), 10.

4

Faith Does Not Continue to Dance On The Foundation

Biblical Perspectives

> *Therefore let us move beyond the elementary teachings about Christ and be taken forward to maturity, not laying again the foundation of repentance from acts that lead to death, and of faith in God, instruction about cleansing rites, the laying on of hands, the resurrection of the dead, and eternal judgment. And God permitting, we will do so* (Hebrews 6:1-3; TNIV).

Both the King James translation and the New Revised Standard Version read: *Let us go on to perfection.* The author in Hebrews is certainly not calling for a life free from fault or error. The better (and I believe more accurate) translation is the challenge to move from the elementary to completion and maturity. The emphasis is clear: there is much more beyond the basics.

Believing that "getting saved" is the final goal of the salvation experience is like attending a Broadway musical and leaving after the overture. The initial commitment is like the curtain going up. It is like the beginning of a journey. It is like the dawning of a new day. It is like life having new perspectives, new visions, new directions, and new goals. It is like being born "from above" (John 3).

In 1 Corinthians 3:1-2 Paul writes this to some people who appear to be stuck in the opening stage of conversion:

> *And so, brothers and sisters, I could not speak to you as spiritual people, but rather as people in the flesh, as infants in Christ. I fed you with milk, not solid food, for you were not ready for solid food.*

The New Living Translation puts it like this: *I had to feed you with milk and not solid food, because you couldn't handle anything stronger.* Paul does not tell these people they have not received God's salvation. He tells them they have not realized the implications of God's grace for the daily living of the life of faith. The Corinthians were not ready for the strong stuff that involved a changed life - becoming new creations in Christ.

> A message the United Church of Christ has been promoting in recent years is: "God is still speaking," The emphasis is on the comma instead of the expected period![38]

A judgment on my part: too many believe that God is the God of periods and not the God of commas. John 16:12-13 bears witness to the God of commas: (Jesus to his disciples) *"I still have many things to say to you, but you cannot bear them now. When the Spirit of truth comes, he will guide you into all the truth..."* The implications are: there is much more to be known and understood; the Spirit will be the on-going teacher; the truths will come as we are open and ready to receive them. I see no indication that there will ever come a time when we will shout, "Got it!" and put a period in our learning. The God of commas continues to speak.

Exploring and Considering

> (Comments after reading Joshua 6:1-27, the story of the conquest of Jericho): It's not always clear what we are meant to

---

38 Michael Dowd, *Thank God for Evolution,* 71.

Faith Never Stands Alone 31

> learn from the Bible's most troubling stories, but if we simply look away, we learn nothing.[39]
>
> The truth is, I've yet to find an explanation for the Bible's war stories that I find completely satisfying.[40]
>
> I don't want to become a person who is unbothered by these texts…There are parts of the Bible that inspired, parts that perplex, and parts that leave you with an open wound. I'm still wrestling, and like Jacob, I will wrestle until I am blessed. God hasn't let go of me yet.[41]

Here is a person who is seeking to go beyond the basic and elementary aspects of faith. She is not content with the bumper sticker I once saw that read: "God said it. I believe it. That settles it." Aside from there being too many periods, this slogan appears to disengage us from one of the most productive aspects of learning: wrestling with Holy Scripture until we wring a blessing out of it (that may not even involve greater understanding). I continue to be disturbed by the "Holy Wars" that called for Israel to completely destroy cities (men, women, and children). Include me among those who have never found an explanation that is completely satisfying. But I continue to wrestle and God hasn't let go of me yet.

Perhaps the temptation to remain with the basic elements of the faith is so strong because once we move forward it involves real effort and hard work – and more:

> Carol Dweck is quick to point out that the growth-mindset advantage "isn't just about effort"; while a willingness to work hard matters, people who want to keep learning "also need to try new strategies and seek input from others when they're stuck."[42]

Faith is always opening new doors and listening to other people (even those who are from different traditions!). Remember the

---

39 Rachel Held Evans, *Inspired* (New York: Nelson Books, 2018), 75.
40 Ibid, 78.
41 Ibid, 79.
42 Hal Gregersen, *Questions Are the Answers* (New York: Harper Business, 2018), 47.

question asked by Nathanael? *"Can anything good come out of Nazareth?"* and the reply given by Philip, *"Come and see."* (John 1:46). My contention is that God's Spirit can speak to us in any situation, at any place, and through any person. We should never limit God's methods of revelation. What we have to do is to be willing to come and see and listen.

> I felt lucky. I'd walked into St. Gregory's right at the moment when Episcopalianism was moving precipitously from the unquestioned center of Establishment power in the United States to the despised periphery. And there, on the edges – as I'd learned before, when I was a student and a cook and a reporter – was where the most interesting truths were to be found.[43]

In Nathanael's day, Nazareth was one of those edges. Even Jesus was perceived by the Scribes and Pharisees of his day as being one of those edges. Wonder what we have missed because we have expected God to speak only in ways in which we expect to hear his Word? It seems to be that throughout Scripture, in so many times and so many ways, it is the God of the edges who has shown up and spoken.

Have you had any "Kodak moments" recently? You don't hear this slogan today because there is no longer any Kodak film in use. Have you ever wondered why it all disappeared?

> In 2012, Kodak found itself in bankruptcy. The destruction took place because someone else had asked and answered the right questions – about how digital technology could transform amateur photography – before Kodak did. This happened despite the fact that in 1974 Kodak engineers had invented the first electronic cameras.[44]

The best comment on this business tragedy is this:

> Many people are aware that to stay healthy the body needs exercise and movement, but few recognize that it is equally important to keep one's thinking in motion. So often we are

---

43 Sara Miles, *Take This Bread* (New York: Ballantine Books, 2007), 89.
44 Hal Gregerson, *Questions Are the Answer*, 48.

satisfied with ideas we picked up years ago and have kept locked up for decades. Our way of looking at the world remains fixed, even as everything in life changes from minute to minute.[45]

I don't know why something I read years ago came immediately to mind: "A text of Scripture is a gate into a large field. Unfortunately, too many ministers spend all their time swinging on the gate." There are always more riches and wisdom in any verse of Scripture than a mere first reading will disclose. It is necessary to wander (contemplate) and explore even the far reaches of the text. There is always much to be discovered and learned if we are brave enough to stop swinging on the gate.

Quotes Worth Thinking About

> Chuck Klosterman's book, *But What If You're Wrong*, points to a "modern culture of certitude." He worries about "our escalating progression toward…ideology that assures people they're right about what they believe. Fighting that culture of certitude is essential because it "hijacks conversation and aborts ideas. It engenders a delusion of simplicity that benefits people with inflexible ideas."[46]

One of my favorite cartoons from *The New Yorker* pictures an announcer in a boxing ring indicating a man behind him who is standing stiffly with arms folded and eyes closed. The announcer is saying, "And in this corner, still undefeated, Frank's long-held beliefs!" You have the feeling he will remain undefeated and your thoughts immediately shift to the similar "undefeated" you know. One of the proven rules of confrontation is: the more you challenge people with entrenched points of view, the more entrenched those views become. You never argue such people into a different position.

The culture of certitude is certainly alive and well during our time. Social media gives people with inflexible ideas lots of ammu-

---
45   Thomas Moore, *Original Self* (New York: HarperCollins, 2001), 102.
46   Hal Gregersen, *Questions Are the Answer*, 115-116.

nition for defending their positions. Some of these certitudes are especially alarming. Pure fear prevents my wandering into the political field where truth and fiction can hardly be separated.

> As is the case with many convenient interpretations of the past, what makes perfect sense is also very often wrong. Squeaky-clean plotlines are simply too convenient to be true.[47]
>
> The gathered wisdom of the library agreed that Luther left from Erfurt in 1510. (They later learned he actually left from Wittenberg.)[48]
>
> We mistook a consensus for a truth and forgot just how murky a thing the past is – even such a simple matter as establishing a date or a place.[49]

The above refers to the decision by Andrew Wilson to attempt, on its five-hundredth-anniversary, to duplicate Martin Luther's thousand mile walk to Rome. The journey was completed in spite of an incorrect assumption. His lesson, that consensus does not necessarily equal truth, is a lesson for all of us. Later we will discuss just how important it is to keep questions at the forefront of our learning. When anyone tells me, "This is what I believe about the matter," I want to ask (and sometimes do), "Based on what?" If the answer is, "My brother-in-law found it on Facebook," I try not to scream. "It is generally believed," or "Most people would agree with me," are not solid bases for determining the truth.

From the novel *Accused* by Lisa Scottoline:

> "You know what they say, 'When you have the law argue the law. When you have the facts, argue the facts. When you don't have either, pound the table.'"[50]

The harder the pounding or the louder the voice has nothing to do with the degree of truth that is being presented. I leave it there for fear of drifting into dangerous territory.

---

47 Andrew L. Wilson, *Here I Walk* (Grand Rapids: Brazos Press, 2016), 3.
48 Ibid, 4.
49 Ibid, 7.
50 Lisa Scottoline, *Accused* (New York: St. Martin's Press, 2013), 146.

COMING TO SOME CONCLUSIONS

Continuing to dance on the foundation of our faith keeps us in safe territory. It saves a lot of struggling, conflict, and thinking. Jesus did not define what the "much more" was that he had to tell his disciples but simply promised them another teacher of truth, the Holy Spirit, who would guide them slowly and carefully, just as Jesus had done, as they were able to receive the lessons (John 16:12-13.)

I agree with what Microsoft's CEO, Satya Nadella, said in an interview in 2016: "The learn-it-all will always triumph over the know-it-all in the long run, even if they start with less innate capability."[51] Jesus' one command to his disciples in what we call "The Great Commission " (Matthew 28:19) is: "make disciples." Make learners, make followers, make students. Make those who never stop being "on the grow."

And, that always means we have to be re-thinking things. (Note: this does not mean we will necessarily have to change everything.) Adam Grant in his excellent book, *Think Again*, contends these are the most annoying things people say instead of rethinking:[52]

1. That will never work here.
2. That's not what my experience has shown.
3. That's too complicated; let's not overthink it.
4. That's the way we've always done it.

I guarantee that this is a perfect formula for continuing to dance on the foundation.

QUESTIONS FOR REFLECTION AND DISCUSSION

1. Do any parts of Scripture make you want to wrestle?

---

51 Alex Beard, *Natural Born Learners* (London: Weidenfeld & Nicolson, 2018), 111.
52 Adam Grant, *Think Again*, 30.

2. What does the "God of the commas" say to you?
3. Have you found any interesting truths on the edges?

5

FAITH IS A KINGDOM WORD

BIBLICAL PERSPECTIVES

> *From that time Jesus began to proclaim, "Repent, for the kingdom of heaven is at hand"* (Matthew 4:17).
>
> *Now after John was arrested, Jesus came to Galilee, proclaiming the good news of God, and saying, "The time is fulfilled, and the kingdom of God has come near: repent, and believe the good news"* (Mark 1:14-15).

To my way of thinking, one of the most interesting (and neglected) questions Jesus ever asked was the one he addressed to the expert in the Mosaic Law who was inquiring about how to gain eternal life. Jesus responds to that question with his question: "*What is written in the law? How do you read it?*" (TNIV). This translation is closer to the Greek than the usual "*What do you read there?*" Jesus was asking, "What kind of perspective do you bring to your reading? What is your frame of reference?" The answers to these questions shed light on why there is so much disagreement and so many divergent interpretations over the same passage of Scripture. We all read WHAT is written; we do not all bring the same HOW to our reading.

I bring this to our attention at the beginning of the chapter because how we read the two texts is largely determined by how we read the words *repent* and *kingdom*. Both John the Baptist and Jesus began their ministries with similar emphases. The phrase "kingdom of God" (same as Matthew's kingdom of heaven) can also be translated as "reign of God" or "realm of God" to distinguish it from an earthly kingdom. Garry Wills gives this helpful insight:

> When Pilate asks if (Jesus) is king, he answers: *"My reign is not of this present order. If my reign were of this order my subjects would be fighting for me, to keep me from arrest by the Jews, but for now my reign is not here"* (John 18:36). Jesus is telling Pilate that he is not a Jewish rebel trying to end Rome's occupation. Pilate nonetheless treats Him as a political figure, nailed the name of his crime on the cross: "Jesus of Nazareth, King of the Jews." It was said earlier that religion killed Jesus. But so did politics – not his own, but that of the earthly realm that fears unearthly claims.[53]

On a regular basis, most of us pray the prayer Jesus gave to his disciples in response to their request: "*Teach us how to pray*" (Luke 11:1). The prayer that Jesus gives is not simply a rote prayer for repetition, but a prayer that underscores the areas in life on which prayer is to focus and what his disciples should emphasize in their praying. The first request in the prayer is: *Thy kingdom come...*" Karen Armstrong defines the prayer as I define it: "The Lord's Prayer is the prayer of the Kingdom"[54] That is the frame of reference by which the prayer is to be understood. To rightly pray what Jesus taught us, we have to put on Kingdom glasses. (More on this later.)

> Jesus proclaims his central message, the Reign of God, in the limit-language not of propositions but of these disruptive, hyperbolic stories.
> In the parables, the proclaimed Reign of God is not a concept. Rather, the Reign of God is what happens in these

---

53 Gary Wills, *What Jesus Meant* (New York: Penguin Books, 2006), 87.
54 Karen Armstrong, *St. Paul: The Apostle We Love to Hate* (Boston: New Harvest, 2015), 7.

unnerving stories told by the disruptive, unsubstitutable Jesus of Nazareth.[55]

David Tracy's use of his word unsubstitutable (he coined it) emphasizes that no one even comes close to what Jesus said and did. Jesus' lack of propositions in talking about the kingdom is replaced by stories. "Most of the major New Testament parables are introduced by the words *"The kingdom of God is like."*[56] Frederick Buechner adds this helpful insight:

> What is the Kingdom of God? Jesus suggests rather than spells out. He evokes rather than explains. He catches by surprise. He doesn't let the homiletic seams show.[57]

The beginning of our understanding of the Kingdom involves repentance – and probably, a new, biblical, understanding of that word.

Exploring and Considering

"Repent!" was a word I often heard from the visiting evangelist at the annual revival in my home church. Unfortunately, it was usually associated with regret and sorrow for past indiscretions and a public display of grief over such shortcomings, frequently on display as people responded to the "invitation" and made their way to the front of the church. The problem is this does not begin to uncover the full meaning of the word.

> The word *metanoeite*…is talking about a primal change of mind, worldview, or your way of processing… Jesus invariably emphasized inner motivation and intention in his moral teaching. He made religion about interior change and "purity of heart" (Matthew 5:8).[58]

---

55 David Tracy, *Fragments* (Chicago: The University of Chicago Press, 2020), 233.
56 Ibid, 335.
57 Frederick Buechner, *Listening to Your Life* (New York: HarperCollins, 1992), 107.
58 Richard Rohr, *The Universal Christ*, 92-93.

While this is true, there may be (and usually is) a degree of regret and commitment to change one's behavior, a change of direction. But Rohr is correct in his assertion that the major thrust of *metanoeite* is a change of worldview and our way of processing. He goes on to say: "Your worldview is not what you look at. It is what you look out from or look through."[59]

Jesus continually called for a Kingdom view and, especially in Matthew, he gave a prescription for the lens. "The Beatitudes are in some sense a Christian's identity card. They identify us as followers of Jesus."[60] I would probably go even further and include the entire Sermon on the Mount in that identity card, as the lenses through which we see and evaluate our lives. When Jesus told Pilate that his reign was not of this order (or world), he had spent up to three years describing the nature of that Kingdom and performing deeds that signaled the Kingdom had arrived.

> (Jesus) says, during his ministry, "*God's reign is in your midst*" (Luke 17:21) …His miracles are meant to prove this: "*If I, with God's touch, cast out devils, then God's reign has arrived*" (Luke 11:20) …God's announcement, the "gospel" normally translated "good news," is precisely the news that the Messiah has arrived.[61]

We've already discussed the faulty translation that has Jesus saying, "*The Kingdom of God is within you,*" which has an appealing ring for the "me generation." The problem is that it makes no sense in the context in which it is presented. In Luke17:20, Jesus is asked by a group of Pharisees when the Kingdom of God would come. Jesus replied: "th*e kingdom of God is in your midst.*" In the text, Jesus points to himself as the kingdom bringer. Would Jesus have told the Pharisees: "*The kingdom of God is within you*"? When you take into account everything Jesus said to the Pharisees or about those in their group who were seeking to end his ministry

---

59 Ibid, 237.
60 Pope Francis, *Happiness in This Life* (New York: Random House, 2017), 67.
61 Gary Wills, *What Jesus Meant*, 84-85.

Faith Never Stands Alone

(and probably his life), one can hardly imagine Jesus telling them that the long-awaited kingdom was in (within) them.

Most Pharisees certainly did not represent the kingdom view, neither did they view life through the principles Jesus talked about. Hal Taussig translates Luke 17:21 – "*the realm of God is among you*" (NEW). I am convinced they knew what Jesus meant and were more determined than ever to eliminate this blasphemer. Jesus accused them of being blind guides; they neither had a kingdom vision, nor could they assist others in directing them how to see and where to look.

Paul Johnson maintains that by his life (and teaching), Jesus provided what was in effect a new Ten Commandments. In his close study of the Gospels, this is what he has come up with:[62]

1. Each of us must develop a true personality. Jesus taught that each of us is unique, and that each has, in addition to a body, a soul in which our character is preserved.
2. Accept, and abide by, universality…Each soul is unique, but is a part of humanity.
3. Respect the fact that we are all equal in God's eyes.
4. The need for love in human relationships, at all time and in every situation.
5. Concern for mercy. We are to show mercy just as God shows it to us…Mercy is grace. It is undeserved.
6. Balance. Seek and maintain a balance in life. Do not go to extremes. Live life in moderation.
7. Cultivate an open mind. Jesus constantly emphasized that dogmatic beliefs, bigotry, and the insistence that there is only one "correct" way of doing, thinking, and talking – as prevalent in his society as in ours – are the exact opposite of truth.
8. The pursuit of truth, whole and unabridged, simple and pure, unadorned by sectarian usage, unstained by passion.
9. The judicious use of power and the respect due the powerless.
10. Show courage in resisting and in enduring wrong.

---

62 Paul Johnson, *Jesus: A Biography From a Believer*, 162-173.

Quotes Worth Thinking About

> If, as the vows in the Episcopal prayer book said, "I believe that the Old and New Testament contain everything necessary for salvation," ...well, sure. I believed the world contained everything necessary for salvation. It was a matter of keeping your eyes open....religion was like learning to see. I was trying to make meaning from things I hadn't previously paid attention to – the events I hadn't bothered to see and the people I didn't want to.[63]

The New Testament translation by David Bentley Hart changes the KJV *"Behold,"* the angel of the Lord appeared to Joseph, (Matthew 2:13) to *"Look": The Lord's angel appears to Joseph in a dream....* This is more in line with Philip's reply to Nathaniel's expressed doubt that anything good could come out of Nazareth: "*Come and see,"* and what Jesus says in Luke 10:23-24: "*Blessed are the eyes that see what you see. For I tell you that many prophets and kings wanted to see what you see but did not see it, and to hear what you hear but did not hear it*" (TNIV). Having eyes that truly see and ears that truly hear is a continuing admonition in Jesus' ministry. Most of us believe we really see but are unaware of how our perspectives are distorted by what we expect to see or want to see. (Note: Hart also changes the *"Verily, verily" of the KJV to:* "Amen, amen," and places it at the beginning of Jesus' sayings: So, Jesus spoke again, "Amen, amen, I tell you"...(Matthew 10:7) which adds a significant note of authority to the teaching.)

> Picasso once said: "There is only one way to see things, until someone shows us how to look at them with different eyes."[64]

It is obvious we are talking about the many worlds of our "seeing": the physical, the spiritual, the intellectual, the emotional.

---

63 Sara Miles, *Take This Bread*, 210-211.
64 Hal Gregersen, *Questions Are the Answer*, 9.

Faith Never Stands Alone

Distorting blindness can often come to light with the insight from another human being. This kind of insight brought about by different eyes can come from anyone, anywhere, and any time. Sara Miles (in the first quote in this section) found it among the "ordinary" people who were helping in her church's program of food distribution for the needy. She was amazed at what people with no formal theological education helped her to see in a totally different way.

> (We) need to read the Bible for formation instead of information.[65]
> We are created to care about what kind of people we are becoming.[66]

When we talk about faith as a Kingdom word, we are talking about the kind of people we are called to be as citizens of that Kingdom. To live by Kingdom ethics will, of necessity, shape us into the kind of people we want to be and certainly the kind of people God wants us to be. This has to do with character and not personality. Even an "excess of personality" (a great line from the Jurassic Park movie) will not make up for character defects. The biggest lesson from the Sermon on the Mount is: Here is the way the followers of Christ are to look. Here is how you will recognize them as people of his Kingdom.

Coming to Some Conclusions

In order to become the kind of people we need to become and to do the things we need to do, we need to keep wearing our Kingdom glasses.

> Psychologist George Kelly observed that our beliefs are like pairs of reality goggles. We use them to make sense of the world and navigate our surroundings.[67]

---

65 Marva Dawn, *In the Beginning, God*, 93.
66 Ibid, 30.
67 Adam Grant, *Think Again*, 127.

What we believe is all important. In the Gospels, the most frequently used title for Jesus is "Teacher." That ties in directly with what we call "The Great Commission" in Matthew 28:19-20 with it's one command – "*make disciples.*" Make learners, make students. (All of the other "commands" are actually participles in the Greek.) This sounds like a radical statement but it has my total agreement (from too many years of classroom instruction!): "The results of education mostly depend on who is teaching them."[68] Jesus was known as an astounding teacher: *All spoke well of him and were amazed at the gracious words that came from his lips* (Luke 4:22; TNIV).

Wouldn't you loved to have been among those who heard Jesus' teachings? In the oral culture of his day, this was the way most people learned (most were illiterate). If you want Scripture to really come alive when you are reading alone, read aloud! It changes everything, even if it is your own voice (perhaps that is why is has such an added impact). Note: "Paul's letters were read aloud, with gestures, mime, and visual aids, to drive a point home. An epistle, therefore, was essentially a speech act and a dramatic performance."[69] Second note: I once heard the Gospel of Mark recited in its totality. My immediately reaction was: "I've never heard that before."

Hearing another voice read to us is a totally different experience from silent reading. Generations ago, even people who read to themselves, read aloud in a low voice. There was very little of what we call "silent reading." Studies show two amazing things:

> The evidence has become so overwhelming that social scientists now consider read-aloud time one of the most important indicators of a child's prospects in life.[70]
>
> We are not even the only species to benefit. Dogs do, too, which is why, since 2014, volunteers at the American Society for the Prevention of Cruelty to Animals have read to animals

---

68 Gary Gutting, *What Philosophy Can Do*, 177.
69 Karen Armstrong, *St. Paul: The Apostle We Love to Hate*, 92.
70 Meghan Cox Gurdon, *The Enchanted Hour* (London: Piatkus, 2019), xiv.

Faith Never Stands Alone

to help them recover from trauma. (The effects of such reading are given on p. 190-191).[71]

It is so easy to forget the comforting, encouraging, blessing, and healing power of the human voice. I've often wondered how many people in Jesus' audience were healed from all kinds of psychological and emotional difficulties simply because they heard his voice. Wearing our Kingdom glasses will help us find the opportunities to speak or read words that will turn around someone's life.

One of the major lessons of this chapter is:

> We are in a very great degree the creators of the reality we inhabit.[72]

QUESTIONS FOR REFLECTION AND CONVERSATION

1. What immediately comes to mind when you hear the term, "The Kingdom of God"?
2. Do you agree with Richard Rohr that "your worldview is not what you look at. It is what you look out from or look through"?
3. What do you think of Paul Johnson's new Ten Commandments?

---

71 Ibid, 189.
72 Marilynne Robinson, *The Givenness of Things* (New York: Farrar, Straus and Giroux, 2015), 234.

6

Faith Is Risky Business

Biblical Perspectives

> *"I am sending you out like sheep among wolves. Therefore be as shrewd as snakes and as innocent as doves."* (Matthew 10:16; TNIV).
>
> *Be alert and of sober mind. Your enemy the devil prowls around like a roaring lion looking for someone to devour.* (1 Peter 5:8; TNIV).

Jesus warns of the wolves and the author of I Peter writes about the danger of a prowling lion. All this comes while the followers of the Way are attempting to carry out God's will for their lives. It appears that the sense of peace and security that Jesus promises us is going to have to be within us; it certainly doesn't sound as though it will be "out there." These are only two of the New Testament red flag notices of the difficulties and risks involved in faithful discipleship. Jesus never promised a risk-free life to those who wanted to follow him. Instead, he talked about counting the cost before one made the decision.

When large crowds began to travel with Jesus, he launched what I like to call an "ensmallment campaign." In Luke 14:25-33, when he talks about counting the cost of becoming his disciple, he includes in that cost placing loyalty to him before loyalty to family and giving up one's possessions. I'll wager not many new recruits signed up that day! "Jesus was a man of the margins, never quite fitting in, always 'out of context.'"[73] Jesus preached a radical faith with radical demands. How else would his followers, as described in the Sermon on the Mount (Matthew 5:13-16), be the salt of the earth and the light of the world?

As many have said before me, if you want a no-risk faith, I urge you to avoid Christianity. However, to be honest, I don't know how you find a risk-free life to begin with. In his magnificent Lord of the Rings, J. R. Tolkein has an early line that provides the context for the three parts of his work:

> "It's a dangerous business, Frodo, going out your front door. You step out on to the road and if you don't keep your feet, there's no knowing where you'll be swept off to."[74]

Life is a risky business. The alternative to no risk is hardly any life at all (I started to put "no life at all" but felt that was too severe). The real issue is whether we intend to take the risk for something that is truly worthwhile. Before undertaking any task, I always ask myself, "Is it worth the risk?" (Yes, even in pastoral ministry, that question was necessary). To seek to avoid risk is on the same table with seeking to avoid conflict. Both are counterproductive to accomplishing the purposes and goals we have for our lives. Neither can be avoided, but both can be dealt with creatively and redemptively and, of course, with faith (confidence that God's grace and guidance will sustain us).

Perhaps it can be said that God never expects from anyone of us what he wouldn't (or doesn't) do himself:

> God is without doubt a great risk taker, and probably that explains the endless and bizarre displays of life we see

---

73 Gary Wills, *What Jesus Really Meant*, xxi.
74 Chris Guillebeaui, *The Happiness of Pursuit* (New York: Harmony, 2014), 13.

Faith Never Stands Alone

on this earth. God is clearly into freedom, imagination, and creativity.[75]

God took the risk of allowing his creation the freedom to live in a garden that contained a forbidden tree. Why not post angelic guards twenty-four-seven around it? Why permit his creation to fully exercise their free-will that was a part of having been created in his image? God took the risk but he never abandoned his supreme creation. He certainly took the risk of allowing the Incarnation to begin, not with a strong and mighty deliverer, but with an infant in a feeding trough. God's risks have always involved a lot of freedom, imagination, and creativity. So should ours.

Exploring and Considering

The risks and scandals of Jesus' earthly ministry should not go unnoticed. They speak to the risk that has always come with his Way.

> It was a source of scandal for women to travel openly with a rabbi: but *"many" women followed Jesus through Galilee* (Luke 8:2-3).[76]
>
> There was a crowd of women followers at the cross, when all but one of the male company had fled or stood far off (Mark 15:40-41). Three of these women who were at the cross were also the first to discover the empty tomb and to announce their finding to the male followers, becoming the first evangels of the Resurrection (Luke 24:1-11). One of these women was the first person to converse with the risen Jesus (John 20:15-17).[77]

Most are aware of this unusual preponderance of women at the cross and the tomb. Many are unaware of, or are reluctant to acknowledge, the preponderance of women among the early of believers. Just check out the role of some of them mentioned by Garry Wills in his excellent *What Jesus Meant*: Chloe (1 Corinthi-

---

75   Richard Rohr, *Immortal Diamond* (San Francisco: Jossey-Bass, 2013), 89.
76   Gary Wills, *What Jesus Meant*, 49.
77   Ibid.

ans 3:11); Phoebe (Romans 16:1); Apphia (Philemon 2); Nympha (Colossians 4:15), Euodia and Syntyche (Philippians 4:3); Lydia (Acts 16:13). (p. 50). Special emphasis is given to two couples:

> Junia is called an emissary (apostolos), Paul's own title for himself. She and her husband shared Paul's imprisonment (Romans 16:7). Prisca and her husband are "my fellow workers, who risked their own necks to save my life," so that the whole assembly owes the two of them its gratitude (Romans 16:3-5). Paul refers to four women – Mary, Tryphaena, Tryphosa, Persis – as having "toiled with effort" (kopiaein, Romans 16:6, 12) for the Christians, the same verb he uses of his own activities (Galatians 4:11, 1 Corinthians 15:10).[78]

If there seems to be a pattern here, you have an eye for the obvious. How is it possible to ignore this list? It takes a lot of exegetical calisthenics to get around what I believe to be such clear texts. I don't believe that is heretical, I believe it is being true to the "totality of the biblical witness" (my favorite phrase describing the secret of better understanding Scripture).

One citation in Gary Will's book was a shocking eye-opener:

> A first-century fresco in the catacomb of Saint Priscilla in Rome shows a woman breaking the eucharistic bread for six other women at the agape table.[79]

All of the above was high risk for a culture in which women did not play a significant role in the life of the synagogue gatherings. The high risk continues in certain denominations but the controversy can be traced far back. "A medieval theologian turned Junia into a man: Andronicus and Junia became Andronicus and Junias. Others at _____ backed it up." (The name of the educational institution is intentionally omitted.)[80]

---

78 Ibid, 50.
79 Ibid, 51.
80 Rachel Held Evans, *A Year of Biblica Womanhood* (Nashville: Nelson Books, 2012), 248.

Quotes Worth Thinking About

> Thomas Merton: "The work of God is never effectively undertaken without daring, without risk.[81]

Whatever your context of involvement with people, you will always get into trouble if you color outside the lines, rock the boat, or go beyond the comfort zone of others. "Play it safe" is the unspoken watchword of many an orthodox keeper of the faith. Thomas Merton is much admired but he certainly had his critics. He knew what it meant to be daring and take risks; his life and writings reveal he did not hesitate to do either. We would certainly be the poorer if he had "played it safe."

My honest confession is, being in a profession where we like to be liked, I don't really look forward to daring and risk. Thank God, it has been thrust upon me many times in my ministry with resulting blessing and accomplishment that never would have come without it. I have found most helpful Hal Gregersen's "Benefits of getting out of your comfort zone":[82]

1. The element of surprise. You encounter the stimulating surprise of bumping into new things and new perspectives.
2. Your focus gets distracted. Stepping away from intense concentration on task puts your mind in a different processing mode, one more receptive to questions that have been lingering at the edge of your consciousness yet eluding you. A classic example is the idea that comes to you in the shower.
3. It gives you the chance to experience unanticipated conflict. (A conflict in perception, emotion, or thought.) That is the most positive kind of conflict, because it involves being hit by an opportunity.

For me, the greatest benefit in getting out of my comfort zone is that I feel more alive. As one gets older, you begin to ask the ques-

---

[81] Thomas Merton, *Mystics and Zen Masters* (New York: Farrar, Straus and Giroux, 1967), 85.
[82] Hal Gregersen, *Questions Are the Answer,* 131-139.

tion captured in a song of years ago, "What's it all about, Alphie?" What is the purpose of life anyway? To play it safe? To avoid the ruffling of any feathers? To keep out of the arenas of conflict and enjoy it from a spectator's spot? To be so well thought of that no one can ever think of any waves created? Result? They probably will not be able to think of many things we ever created! (This is preaching and I know it, so please pardon the pulpit pounding!)

When Jesus told people to count the cost before they decided to follow him, it was something well understood by his listeners. It is not so obvious to most of us in our modern world.

> The fact that ancient gods ran in the blood meant that people were born into their obligations to particular deities – family gods, civic gods, and (a special case) imperial gods. If these pagans became Christ-followers, ceasing to honor their gods with cult, they risked alienating heaven and thereby endangering their city…At issue was not "belief" – everyone knew these superhuman powers existed – but the public display of respect.
> Divine wrath risked havoc: gods struck with flood or famine, with drought and disease; they could level cities with earthquakes or allow foreign armies to invade.[83]

Now it is easy to understand why some early Christians were called atheists. They did not offer sacrifices or respect to the local gods who, if not placated, could easily wreak all kinds of havoc.

Coming To Some Conclusions

If Christianity is to be "the way, the truth, and the life," there is no way it can be risk free. Risk is a part of being alive, of living in a real world, and of participating in that world. Certainty is not the watchword for such a life, nor should it be:

> Too much certainty is boring, unrewarding and belittling…This is not to say that we should all sign up to become

---

83   Paula Frederikson, *Paul: The Pagans' Apostle*, 89-90.

tightrope walkers or war photographers, but we ought to recognize that opportunities is life necessarily involve taking risks, and that too much caution might not be good for our existential health...For now it is worth recalling a phrase we often hear children saying to one another: "I dare you."[84].

QUESTIONS FOR REFLECTION AND DISCUSSION

1. Do you believe that faith is risky business? Why is this so?
2. Do you believe "God is a great risk taker?"
3. Are you surprised at the number of women mentioned in Scripture as early Believers?

---

84 Roman Krznartic, *Carpe Diem Regained* (London: Unbound, 2017), 82.

7

FAITH ALWAYS INVOLVES ACTION

BIBLICAL PERSPECTIVES

Dear brothers and sisters, what's the use of saying you have faith is you don't prove it by your actions? That kind of faith can't save anyone. (James 2:14, NLT).

So you see, it isn't enough just to have faith. Faith that doesn't show itself by good deeds is no faith at all – it is dead and useless. (James 2:17, NLT).

Fool! When will you ever learn that faith that does not result in good deeds is useless?... Just as the body Is dead without a spirit, so also faith is dead without good deeds. (James 2:20, 26 NLT).

Some have accused the author of James of pitching a fit in his section about the relationship between faith and works. It probably couldn't begin to compare with the fit Martin Luther pitched with his reaction in calling the work "a rather strawy epistle." The letter was probably written to Jewish Christians scattered throughout the Roman empire and James is most concerned about the impact their faith will have on the "pagan" world. He must have firmly believed in the old adage: "actions speak louder than words." He maintains that it was the actions of Abraham that revealed the depths of his faith. He goes so far as to say: *Was not our ancestor Abraham justified by works when he offered his son Isaac on the altar?* (James 2:21). If you stop reading with this verse, you will miss the larger context in which it is placed. Here is verse 22: *You see that faith was active along with his works and faith was brought to completion by the works.*

It is easy to see how a new faith with the watchword, "All you have to do is have faith," could quickly become distorted into an easy religion that doesn't call for a lot of effort. Ephesians 2:8-9 can easily be misunderstood: *For by grace you have been saved through faith and this is not your own doing, it is the gift of God – not the result of works, so that no one may boast.* Years ago, I remember hearing a song with the line, "I'm rocking my way to heaven in that easy rocking chair." Unable to recall anything else, it sounded too much like someone who had ticket in hand for the Glory Express and was simply waiting for the arrival of transportation to God's celestial realm.

I Thessalonians 1:3 gives a more pastoral approach to the relationship between faith and works: *We remember before our God and Father your work produced by faith, your labor prompted by love, and your endurance inspired by hope in our Lord Jesus Christ* (TNIV). I also like the way the Greek text is captured in the translation by David Bentley Hart: *Remembering the work of your faithfulness and the labor of your love and the patience of your hope in our Lord Jesus the Anointed before our God and Father…*

> What did Jesus historically have in mind when he said "follow me" as he did so often – creed or behavior? More often than not, I believe Jesus called for response – action to his teaching instead of words or otherwise putting on some kind of show for others.[85]

This certainly is in line with the crash that concludes The Sermon on the Mount. Jesus ends the sermon with the story of two builders. One builds on a solid foundation of rock. When storms and floods come, the house stands. The other builder is foolish and erects the house on sand. When the storms and floods arrive,

---

85 Walt Shelton, *The Daily Practice of Life* (Rapid City, SD: CrossLink Publishing, 2020), 62.

the house comes crashing down. Jesus explains that the first is the person who listens to his teaching and acts on it. The second is the person who listens to his teaching and does not act on it (Matthew 7:24-27).

In Luke's version of the story, found in what we call "The Sermon on the Plain," Jesus introduces the parable with the question: *"Why do you call me 'Lord, Lord,' and do not do what I tell you?"* (Luke 6:46). Nowhere is there any indication that Jesus ever separates faith from works. He actually says the same thing as the later author of James will say, *"If your faith doesn't result in action, it doesn't stand the test of true faith. It cannot stand alone"* (James 2:17).

Exploring And Considering

If you are regular reader of the Psalms, you know that hardly any area of life is left untouched. There are hymns of adoration, praise, and thanksgiving; but there are also many "Psalms of lament." Life is seen as disappointing and God doesn't appear to be doing his job in keeping the scales of justice balanced. Psalm 94 is one long lament over the deeds of the wicked and God's inaction: *How long, O Lord? How long will the wicked be allowed to gloat?* 94:3. In Psalm 37, the writer (usually attributed to David) is encouraging those who can't understand why the wicked seem to be getting away with so much.

I like Psalm 37 because it gives a plan of action to follow while the wicked appear to be having their day. (Verses from the NLT):

1. *Trust in the Lord and do good (vs. 3).*
2. *Take delight in the Lord (vs. 4).*
3. *Commit everything you do to the Lord. Trust him and he will help you (vs.5).*
4. *Be still in the presence of the Lord, and wait patiently for him to act (vs. 7).*
5. *Stop your anger! Turn from your rage (vs. 8).*
6. *Turn from evil and do good (vs. 27).*

7. *Don't be impatient for the Lord to act! Travel steadily along his path (vs. 34).*

This seems in lockstep with Paul's advice to Christians living in a Roman-controlled world: *Never be conquered by evil, but conquer evil with good* (Romans 12:21). In the verses preceding this he gives some concrete examples: blessing in return for cursing, refusing to take revenge, giving your hungry enemy food, and giving your thirsty enemy water. This seems to me a corollary to Micah 6:8 (NLT): *No, O people, the Lord has already told you what is good, and this is what he requires: to do what is good, to love mercy, and to walk humbly with your God.*

When I was an adjunct professor at a seminary, I had a large class each semester called The Exit Class. Its purpose was to assist students in making the transition from a life focused on classroom learning to one focused on ministry with people. I tried to introduce the students to the areas they would need to consider in this frequently jarring adjustment. In a discussion one day about reading, a student proudly announced, "I never read fiction. I read books from which I can learn something."

There are all kinds of reasons to read good fiction (and some fun "beach" reading as well), but I let the class know that I had learned a great deal about life and people from the fiction I had read. The fiction reading and the learning continues to this day. From the novel *I Am Pilgrim* by Terry Hayes, comes this thoughtful insight:[86]

> In the stillness of the night two lines from an old poem whose name or author I couldn't remember drifted into my head:
> I slept and dreams that life was beauty;
> I woke, and found that life was duty.
> Life was duty. Like any soldier going into battle, I thought of the conflict that lay ahead. To be honest, I didn't hope for

---

86   Terry Hayes, *I Am Pilgrim* (New York: Emily Bestle, 2017), 2.

success or glory. I just hoped that I would acquit myself with honor and courage.

The words "honor" and "courage" coming in the context of this story say much more than the simple mandate: To fully live the Christian life we need honor and courage. The impact of the words in a story is multiplied a hundred-fold.

Frequently, an old idea needs to be revisited with fresh insight. Roman Krznaric, in *Carpe Diem Regained* does just that. His sub-title is: The Vanishing Art of Seizing the Day. Here are a couple of excerpts:

> Carpe diem – seize the day – is one of the oldest philosophical mottos in Western history. First uttered by the Roman poet Horace over 2,000 years ago, it retains an extraordinary resonance in popular culture.[87]
>
> Deep-rooted forces have ousted the carpe diem ideal Just Do It and supplanted it with a new set of aspirations: Just Plan It, Just Buy It, Just Watch It and (in a later chapter brought by the mindfulness movement) Just Breathe. [88]

COMING GO SOME CONCLUSIONS

> Truth is not, in fact, propositional...Saint Augustine proposed the concept he called *facere veritatem*. This roughly translates as "doing the truth" or "making the truth happen."[89]

The verse of Scripture that immediately comes to mind is Psalm 86:11: *Teach me your way, O Lord, that I may WALK in your truth...* Another great action text is Psalm 37:3 – *Trust in the Lord and DO good.*

---

87 Roman Krznaric, *Carpe Diem Regained,* 2.
88 Ibid, 47.
89 Christian Platt, *Post Christian* (New York: Jericho Books, 2014), 43.

Openness to the transforming Spirit will ensure that "The Way," as the movement that formed around Jesus was originally called, will never become "the Stay."[90].

When Paul lists the fruits of the Spirit in Galatians 5:22-23, they reflect not only the transforming work of the spirit but are attributes that must be demonstrated in the way one lives: *love, joy, peace, patience, kindness, goodness, trustfulness, gentleness, and self-control.* If I were to tell you that some of the most orthodox people I have known have not been the nicest people in the world to be around, you would probably say, "Amen." Jesus knew some people like that in his day – they were called Pharisees (big note: that certainly did not include ALL Pharisees).

A helpful insight into a life of Christian action comes from Malcolm Muggeridge in his classic account of Mother Teresa's ministry, *Something Beautiful for God*:

> Criticism of Mother Teresa is often directed at the insignificant scale of the work she and the Sisters undertake by comparison with the need…But then Christianity is not a statistical view of life.[91]

Much of what follows will address the what, where, and how of our actions as people of faith. However, I use the following now even though it could just as easily fit in another category:

> There's way too much emphasis on thinking and way too little emphasis on doing. Instead of seeing creativity as "think, think, think, think, think," followed by "do, do, do, do, do," we needed to understand it as a cycle, "thinking and doing, thinking and doing, thinking and doing." If I'd been taught then that the best work took hundreds of drafts, was a process requiring failure after failure, with slight improvements as you progressed through it, I'd have been much better prepared for

---

90 Tom Stell, *A Faith Worth Believing*, 60.
91 Malcolm Muggeridge, *Something Beautiful for God* (San Francisco: Harper & Row, 1971), 28.

the world outside school. And I might have written this book a bit sooner.[92]

Questions For Reflection and Conversation

1. Have you ever considered the reason given in this chapter for the crash that ends the Sermon on the Mount?
2. Have you considered Psalm 37 a prescription for dealing with the apparent prosperity of the wicked?
3. What do you think about Augustine's concept of "doing the truth" or "making the truth happen"?

---

92 Alex Beard, *Natural Born Learners*, 130.

8

Faith and Perseverance Move In Lockstep

Biblical Perspectives

> *...let us run with perseverance the race that is set before us...* (Hebrews 12:1).
>
> *Rejoice in hope, be patient in suffering, persevere in prayer* (Romans 12:12).
>
> *For you need endurance, so that when you have done the will of God, you may receive what he has promised* (Hebrews 10:36).
>
> *(Love) bears all things, believes all things, hopes all things, endures all things* (1 Corinthians 13:7).

Any concordance quickly indicates how saturated the Bible is with calls for perseverance and endurance (both meaning: "hang in there"). Perseverance is certainly one of the many biblical mountaintops.

The benefits of almost anything are quickly lost if one is not willing to stick with it for a reasonable (and, often, an unreasonable) amount of time. One of things any business looks for in a perspective employee is the ability to stick with a task, especially when the going gets rough. The ability to complete a task is one of the basic characteristics of successful people in almost any field. That also holds true for prayer.

According to Jesus, by far the most important thing about praying is to keep at it.[93]

In Luke 11:5-10, Jesus tells the parable of a person who, at a late hour, is surprised by a sudden out-of-town guest. With the cupboard bare, she rushes next door, awakens her neighbor and asks for the loan of three loaves of bread. The neighbor does not wish to disturb the rest of the household, and at first refuses the request. Jesus then comes to the point:

> *"I tell you that even though she will not get up and give her anything because she is a friend, yet because of her persistence she will rouse herself and give her what she wants.*
>
> *"And so I say to you: Ask, and it will be given you; search, and you will find; knock, and the door will be opened to you. For the person who asks receives, everyone who searches finds, and to the person who knocks the door will be opened to you."*

This emphasis on persistence in prayer involves a lot of unpacking, but a couple of things are more than obvious. Our praying is a "keep on keeping on" experience. Many have suggested diverse reasons for this: the specifics and direction of our request may change over time; in the process we may be changed in subtle or dramatic ways. Whatever the reason for this emphasis, the lesson is clear: we must be persistent in our praying if we are expecting results (and those results may not be the ones we were asking for in the beginning).

Ask, seek, and knock are also found in "The Sermon on the Mount." William Barclay calls the section in which it is found, "The Charter of Prayer," and he uses the correct tenses of the three verbs (but, alas, also only masculine pronouns):[94]

> *Keep on asking, and it will be given you;*
> *Keep on seeking, and you will find;*
> *Keep on knocking, and it will be opened to you.*

---

93 Frederick Buechner, *Listening to Your Life*, 212.
94 William Barclay, *The Gospel of Matthew*, Vol 1 (Philadelphia: The Westminster Press, 1958), 273-274.

Faith Never Stands Alone

> *And he who seeks finds;*
> *And to him who knocks it will be opened.*
>
> *What man is there, who, if his son will ask him for bread, will give him a stone? Or, if he will ask for a fish, will he give him a serpent? If then, you, who are grudging, know how to give good gifts to your children, how much more will your Father in heaven give good things to those who ask Him?* (Matthew 7:7-11).

Both Barclay's translation and commentary speak clearly to the basic meaning of Jesus' lesson on prayer.

> Any man who prays is bound to want to know to what kind of God he is praying.[95]
>
> There is a lesson here: God will always answer our prayers; but he will answer them in His way, and His way will be the way of perfect and of perfect love. Often if He answered our prayers as we at the moment desire, it would be the worst thing possible for us, for in our ignorance we often ask for gifts which would be our ruin. This saying of Jesus tells us, not only that God will answer, but that God will answer in wisdom and in love.[96]

In our asking, we may discover other concerns that alter the content of what we ask; in our seeking we make discoveries that have nothing to do with our original quests; in our knocking, we may find other doors opening that we didn't know even existed. For me, prayer is a time for discovery, self-awareness, and openness to new possibilities. I ask, seek, and knock with the limited knowledge and perspective that is mine as a human being. Persistent praying often means a refinement of what I want, what I am looking for, and what needs to be made available for me to move ahead.

Exploring and Considering

From *The Nine Taylors:* He remained lost in melancholy thought for some minutes, and Wimsey did not interrupt him.

---

95 Ibid, 274.
96 Ibid, 274-276.

Then he spoke, weightily, and with long years of endurance in his voice. (A sluice-keeper in response to a question by Lord Peter Wimsey).[97]

You'll never meet a better mystery writer (*The Nine Taylors* is considered by many to be her finest literary achievement) or a better theologian (you can understand!) than Dorothy Sayers. The Lord Peter Wimsey series is a great read with insights like the one above. Nowhere else have I heard a phrase on wisdom to equal: "Then he spoke, weightily, and with long years of endurance in his voice." The weight of the sluice-keeper's reply came because of years of doing and continuing to learn his task. His response was not that of "beginner's luck" but of experienced know-how. To get weight in our speech requires more than smatterings from the experts or a moderate amount of time spent in an endeavor. After sixty years of pastoral ministry, I feel I am just beginning to graduate from a "light-weight" to, at least, "not quite so light-weight."

Dorothy Sayers (1893-1957) is as rewarding in her theological writings as she is in her works of fiction. Her persistence as a writer is revealed in the great diversity of her talents as a writer of poetry, mysteries, plays, short stories, literary criticism, and essays. She was especially proud of her translation of Dante's *Divine Comedy*.

One of her classic theological works is *The Mind of the Maker*. Although issued in 1941, it is as fresh and current as anything you will ever read on such subjects as the image of God, the Trinity, free will, and evil. A second recommendation is a compilation by Laura K. Simmons, exploring theology in Sayers' writings. The title is *Creed Without Chaos*. Three snippets will let you know something of the richness and variety in this book:

> One of Sayer's first jobs was in advertising. She is credited with coining the phrase, "It pays to advertise."[98]

---

[97] Dorothy L. Sayers, *The Nine Taylors* (London: Hodder & Stoughton, 1968), 187.

[98] Laura Simmons, *Creed Without Chaos* (Grand Rapids: Baker Academic, 2005), 46.

Sayers wrote in 1952 that Christianity "is not primarily an emotional experience, or a set of logical conclusions, or a code of ethics: it is a story."[99]

"A great many religious difficulties arise out of entirely misconceived and mistaken notions of what Christian doctrine actually is." Sayers wrote that she found herself often required to defend Christianity against not only atheists and others outside the church but also what she called "slip-slop and fiddle-faddle."[100]

The values of perseverance are not only evident in what we do, but, perhaps, more important in who we are: "Character consists of what you do on the third and fourth tries" (James A. Michener). Most worthwhile things in life do not come quickly or easily. Through the practice of perseverance, we build into our lives (and character) one of the traits that pays exceptional dividends. Note the emphasis on the word "practice." N. T. Wright makes a strong case for praying and living the Psalms every day to achieve any significant impact on our lives. A haphazard, occasional reading will not be sufficient.

Wright says that is like the soccer player who still expects to score goals in games without ever showing up for practice. The Psalms are the steady, sustained subcurrent of healthy Christian living. They shaped the praying and vocation even of Jesus himself. They can and will do the same for us.[101]

To achieve perseverance in other areas of life, I believe it is essential to lay the groundwork of regular, scheduled Scripture reading, prayer, and meditation. Giving twenty to thirty minutes to this discipline will provide a substructure that will undergird you through the challenges of each day. Start with ten minutes if this sounds too demanding but, I ask, what other preparation could better prepare us for daily living? If we want to score goals in the game of life, there must be endless hours of preparing ourselves for

---

99 Ibid, 49.
100 Ibid, 61.
101 Ibid, 61.

the times when opportunities arise. No last-minute effort or struggle will compensate for the lack of disciplined practice. The catch is that we have to decide what it means in our lives to score goals.

Coming to Some Conclusions

> *Let us not become weary in doing good, for at the proper time we will reap a harvest if we do not give up* (Galatians 6:9, TNIV).

The matching secular quote is from Jim Rohn: "How long should you try? Until…" The only acceptable deadline for our work is "until…." In Galatians, it is until there is a harvest of the planting we have done. That "until" varies according to the kind of planting we are doing, but applies to all our efforts:

> Tom Wolfe: Your main problem as a reporter is, simply, managing to stay with whatever you are writing about long enough for the scenes to take place before your eyes."[102]

As with so many things in life, the secret of success is not so much inspiration as it is perspiration! Whenever I am asked, "Where do you get your inspiration for writing?", I always give the same answer: I don't wait for inspiration to strike before I begin writing. I place myself before the computer's blank screen and begin to write. If nothing begins to flow, I simply sit and think. Inspired writing is usually nothing less than the dogged work of staying at it "long enough for the scenes to take place before one's eyes." Some days it will flow almost effortlessly, others will be labored and almost painful. The secret: keep at it on a regular time, on a regular basis. And then there is always the re-writing and the re-writing and the re-writing. The first writing is always a "going with the flow," which means ignoring structure, spelling, or continuity. There is almost total freedom at this stage of writing. The tough stuff comes with the editing.

---

[102] Frye Gaillard, *The Books That Mattered* (Montgomery: NewSouth Books, 2012), 68.

Thomas Edison continues to be one of my perseverance models: "Our greatest weakness lies in giving up. The most certain way to succeed is always to try just one more time."

Questions for Reflection and Conversation

1. Were you surprised by the verb tenses in Matthew 7?
2. How do you attempt to speak "weightily"?
3. Why is perseverance so important in every area of life?

9

Faith and Courage Are Tightly Bound Together

Biblical Perspectives

> *I have said this to you, so that you may have peace. In the world you face persecution. But take courage: I have conquered the world!* (John 16:33).
>
> *Wait for the Lord; be strong, and let your heart take courage; wait for the Lord!* (Psalm 27:14).
>
> *The believers from there (Rome), when they heard of us, came as far as the Forum of Appius and Three Taverns to meet us. On seeing them, Paul thanked God, and took courage* (Acts 28:15).

The more one investigates the biblical dimensions of faith, the stronger and more comprehensive the word becomes. Faith and courage are so intertwined that it is often difficult to separate one from the other. That courage has several sources: (1) It comes from Jesus' teaching and the assurance of the fulfillment of God's purposes of redemption and is evidenced by the sense of well-being (Shalom, peace) that is his gift to his followers; (2) It comes from the hopeful waiting for God's timing and intervention; (3) It comes from among the community of believers who have Barnabas as their patron saint: *There was a Levite, a native of Cyprus, Joseph, to whom the apostles gave the name Barnabas* (which means "son of encouragement"), Acts 4:36.

There is an abundance of biblical evidence suggesting that the opposite of faith is not doubt, but fear. When the disciples awaken a sleeping Jesus over their alarm at a sinking boat, after rebuking the wind and calming the sea, he asks them: *"Why are you afraid? Have you still no faith?"* (Mark 4:40). That fear demonstrates a lack of courage as some other translations indicate: *"Why are you cowards? Do you not have faith?* (BARNSTONE). *"Why are you so cowardly? Have you no faith?"* (SCHONFIELD).

The cowardly lion in *The Wizard of Oz* is not the only one who keeps looking for courage and hoping that a great and mighty wizard will be able to supply it. After a frantic search and the defeat of the wicked witch of the East, the wizard tells the lion that the courage he has been seeking is within him. He gives him a medal so he won't forget. Like so many of the things we seek (peace, security, harmony, etc.), we ultimately will find them only within ourselves. That is the location for faith, hope, and love. Jesus never placed the peace he promised in ideal circumstances; he placed it in the hearts and lives of his disciples. The hope they longed for came as they incorporated in their thinking and living the promises Jesus gave them. The love they so sought sprang within as they opened their hearts to God's love sent their way through his son.

My firm belief is that Jesus kept all these things in his own life and ministry because he spent so much time in prayer, meditation, and saturating himself with the words of Scripture. He did not travel "lightly" in his ministry; he carried everything within that enabled him to meet every circumstance with faith and courage. That is why he had so much to give; he had so much stored within himself. Out of this abundance he continued to give. Courage was not only in his travelling bag, it was in his heart. It took the disciples a long time to learn that faith and courage were things the world could never give them and it was useless to keep looking for them "out there."

EXPLORING AND CONSIDERING

Paul Tillich liked to use the term "the courage to be." This is the essence of faith; it has to do with the will to affirm life and its goodness despite all doubts, difficulties, and sufferings.[103]

I would label courage the "in spite of" word. That would correlate with what Plato wrote in the *Laches:* "Perhaps courage is "wise endurance."[104] The courage to be with wise endurance might be a good definition for faith in a world of challenges. I recently re-watched the movie *Miss Potter*, the story of Beatrix Potter and her animal stories, the most famous of which is *Peter Rabbit.* I remember reading these to my sons when they were small; the pictures especially captivated their young eyes. The story of the author is as fascinating as the characters in her books.

Beatrix Potter (1866-1943) grew up in a man's world and faced masculine-dominated publishers and a mother who had classical Victorian ideas about what was proper for her daughter; supervising the printing of her first book was not on the list. Beatrix demonstrated the courage of wise endurance in insisting on filling her book with pictures and making it affordable. The publishers, except for the one who worked with her, thought the book would sell only a few copies. *The Tale of Peter Rabbit* was published in 1902 when she was thirty-six. By the end of the year. twenty-eight thousand copies were in print. She wrote a total of twenty-three books. Her success enabled her to buy a farm in the Lake District. With additional acreage added through the years, at her death she left over four-thousand acres to the National Trust.

As you watch the movie, you are amazed at the courage this young girl (and, later, young woman) exhibited in the face of such continuing opposition to her hopes and dreams. She demonstrated wise endurance every step of the way even with the tragic loss of her fiancé. She later was married for thirty years to her childhood friend who had become a solicitor in the Lake District.

---

103 Kenneth S. Long, *The Zen Teachings of Jesus,* 134.
104 Atul Gwande, *Being Mortal* (New York: Metropolitan Books, 2014), 233.

I know that every story of faith does not have what can be called a "happy" ending. The "Don't worry, everything will be okay," doesn't always turn out that way. Perhaps that is why it takes so much courage to maintain faith and hope when "they lived happily ever after" cannot be the last line. What can always be the last line for those with faith and courage as wise endurance is: "they lived truly blessed lives all their days" (the kind of blessings so aptly described in the Beatitudes of Matthew chapter five).

In describing Mother Teresa, here is what Brian Kolodiejchuk, the editor of a book of her writings, says of those who worked with her:

> Her superiors and companions had by now become acquainted with her prayerfulness, compassion, charity, and zeal; they also appreciated her great sense of humor and natural talent for organization and leadership. In all her endeavors she consistently showed unusual presence of mind, common sense, and courage, such as when she chased away a bull on the road in order to protect her girls and when she scared off thieves who broke into the convent one night.[105]

Where in her job description (if she had one) was there mention of getting a bull off a street in Calcutta or confronting thieves who were breaking into the convent? Many (could I say most?) of the things we are called on to deal with in our daily lives are not in any job description, but they are in descriptions of what I call Life-101. Why? Perhaps this is the reason:

> The desire of God for us and in us has everything to do with our development as whole persons, and therefore with our willingness to engage reality whether we like it or not.[106]

That quote comes the book titled *A Faith Worth Believing*. Any faith worth believing will involve our development as whole persons. It certainly is not something that can be isolated to our

---

105 Mother Teresa, Brian Kolodiejchuk, ed., *Come Be My Light*, (New York: Doubleday, 2007), 19.
106 Tom Stell, *A Faith Worth Believing*, 85.

Faith Never Stands Alone

"spiritual development" (whatever that is supposed to mean). In my books, spiritual development has to do with everything we are as human beings and every phase of our existence. A faith that shields us from reality or denies reality is not biblical faith. What kind of biblical and theological books do I read? Rachel Held Evans speaks for me:

> The biblical scholars I love to read don't go to the holy text looking for ammunition with which to win an argument or trite truisms with which to escape the day's sorrows, they go looking for a blessing, a better way of engaging life and the world, and they don't expect to escape that search unscathed.[107]

QUOTES WORTH THINKING ABOUT

> Winston Churchill: Success is not final; failure is not fatal: it is the courage to continue that counts.[108]

Success is not the sign that it is time to coast for the rest of life, it is a signal that something greater might now be possible. In the life of faith, success is never a signal to write "The End" to our journey, it is the indication of a crossroad and of the need to make a decision about the direction in which we are to go. We need to be reminded that failure is not fatal; it certainly is not the time to put a period at the end of our efforts, but rather to place a comma and think about what can and should come next in the light of (and in spite of) our failure. More about this in chapter sixteen.

> I discovered I could focus less on the externals and stop trying to hide my symptoms. This was in stark relief from my days on *Spin City* when I'd keep a live audience waiting while I paced in my dressing room, pounding my arm with my fist in a vain attempt to quell the tremors. On *Scrubs,* instead of trying to kill it, I invited Parkinson's with me to the set.

---

107 Rachel Held Evans, *Inspired,* 28.
108 Isaac Lidsky, *Eyes Wide Open* (New York: A TarcherPerigee Book, 2017), 75.

I can play anyone, as long as they have Parkinson's. And as I was discovering, *everyone has Parkinson's*.[109]

This courage to face and live with our challenges (disabilities) out in the open, probably comes as a surprise to many. Hiding our weaknesses has usually been the rule of the day. The irony is that sooner or later most people discover what it is we are attempting to hide. Aside from the fact that it takes so much energy to hide our "tremors" (whatever form they might take), it only makes sense to apply that wasted energy to the task at hand. The courage to continue even in the light of the Parkinson's *we all have,* is having a worth-while faith and may just be the kind of faith that overcomes the world (I John 5:4).

COMING TO SOME CONCLUSIONS

Walt Shelton in *The Daily Practice of Life* has many memorable lines, including this one: "There is a marked difference between feeling fear and choosing to be afraid."[110] That stance of faith can be chosen over the stance of being afraid even though life may so challenge us at times that we feel fear. Somewhere I read that there are 365 "fear nots" in the Bible, one for every day in the year. I haven't counted but there are enough to let me know we are counseled not to live in the fear mode but in the faith mode. The moments of fear are meant to be little blips in our basic stance when something (or someone) catches us off-guard and momentarily shatters our sense of shalom. We can't choose never to have times when fear gains an upper hand, but we can choose not to be dominated by it. How can this be achieved?

One of the best methods I know is to keep ever in mind the nature of the God who calls us to the life of faith.

---

109 Michael J. Fox, *No Time Like the Future* (New York: Flatiron Books, 2020), 24-25.
110 Walt Shelton, *The Daily Practice of Life,* 38.

Faith Never Stands Alone

> Lamentations 3:22 – *The steadfast love of the Lord never ceases, his mercies never come to an end; they are new every morning; great is your faithfulness.*

God's love, mercy, and faithfulness are his continuing gifts that are meant to enable us to live lives of courage and hope. Our faith, hope, love, and courage come in response to God's first bestowing them on us. *There is no fear in love, but perfect love casts out fear… We love because he first loved us* (I John 4:18-19). Our God is the God of initiative; he always makes the first move. Jesus sums up his ministry in Luke 19:10 – *"The Son of Man came to seek and to save the lost."* God is the one who seeks, all we have to do is to allow ourselves to be found.

Our faith and courage do not ultimately rest with us but are focused on the One whose very nature it is to be faithful, even when we are not. Every morning we need to take time to realize the gifts of God's love, mercy, and faithfulness which are daily renewed.

Questions For Reflection and Conversation

1. Can you envision courage as "wise endurance"?
2. Do you believe that faith, hope, and courage are within us and not "out there"?
3. What do you think about Michael J Fox's decision not to hide his Parkinson's?

10

Faith Does Not Protect Us from Life's Difficulties and Tragedies

Biblical Perspectives

> *Now faith is the assurance of things hoped for, the conviction of things not seen. Indeed, by faith our ancestors received approval* (Hebrews 11:1).
>
> *Others were tortured, refusing to accept release, in order to obtain a better resurrection. Others suffered mocking and flogging, and even chains and imprisonment. They were stoned to death, they were sawn in two, they were killed by the sword; they went about in skins of sheep and goats, destitute, persecuted, tormented – of whom the world was not worthy. They wandered in deserts and mountains, and in caves and holes in the ground* (Hebrews 11:35-38).

After the author of Hebrews mentions the accomplishments of some on the "roll call of faith," he then adds the above section which portrays the dark side of that faith. The list of the things that happened to many of the faithful makes you want to ask, "Could I sign up for another division in the Kingdom?" Unfortunately, there are no other divisions. Most of us will never experience what happened to many in the early years of the Christian movement, but we will never be able to count on a utopian existence.

Here, from three different translations of John 16:33, is Jesus' classic bad news/good news:

I have told you all this so that you may have peace in me. Here on earth you will have many trials and sorrows. But take heart, because I have overcome the world (NLT).

I have told you all this so that you may find peace in me. In the world you will have trouble, but be brave: I have conquered the world (JB).

I have said this to you, so that in me you may have peace. In the world you face persecution. But take courage: I have conquered the world (NRS).

In the Hebrew Scriptures, one of the major signs that a false prophet (almost always associated with the established powers) was speaking, was the assurance that all was well and that there was no trouble or judgment coming. True prophets usually came on the scene because of a needed course correction in the lives of the people and the nation. The classic confrontation between a true prophet of God and false prophets, was between Jeremiah, who warned of coming exile, and those termed "lying" prophets:

Then I said, "Ah, Lord God! Here are the prophets saying to them, 'You shall not see the sword nor shall you have famine, but I will give you true peace in this place.'" And the Lord said to me, The prophets are prophesying lies in my name; I did not send them, nor did I command them or speak to them. They are prophesying to you a lying vision, worthless divination, and the deceit of their own minds (Jeremiah 14:13-14).

Jeremiah gave a message no one wanted to hear; the lying prophets told the people what was contrary to the plain writing on the wall, but what they readily believed in spite of circumstances to the contrary. Amos got applause when he began his message with a series of judgments on Israel's neighbors but when Israel became the target of God's disfavor, Amaziah, the priest of Bethel, told Amos, "*O seer, go, flee away to the land of Judah, earn your bread there, and prophesy there; but never again prophesy at Bethel, for it is the king's sanctuary, and it is a temple of the kingdom"* (Amos 7:12-13). Kings and temples do not mean immunity from sorrow, tragedy, and judgment.

Exploring and Considering

> Difficulties are a fact of life. Many of us create unnecessary suffering for ourselves because we expect life to be easy and fail to see our own limitations as mortals. Thus, we try to do the impossible, control the uncontrollable, and predict the unpredictable. We also have the illusion that if we try hard enough, we can secure a problem-free life. Our suffering is the combined result of our ignorance and our inner violence.[111]

Acceptance of the fact (and it *is* a fact) that life is difficult is the beginning of being able to receive the peace that Jesus promised to give us. Somewhere I read about the person who said, "I have decided to cooperate with the inevitable." Not everyone makes that decision. Many still insist that there is a "secret" out there somewhere that will enable them to eliminate (or greatly reduce) the troubles and tragedies of life. There is not a single verse of Scripture that conveys such a promise. Instead, the Bible is filled with prescriptions for how to deal with the dark side of life without falling victim to despair.

The only place to begin in dealing with the negatives of life is the simple acknowledgment that they are built into the reality of existence. "As Camus remarked, 'The crushing truths perish from being acknowledged.'"[112] I'm not certain that they perish but I am certain that they lose much of their power. When we acknowledge that "No road is without bumps",[113] we are much better prepared for any journey we take on the highway of life. Every jolting encounter with those bumps does not traumatize us;

---

[111] Kenneth S. Long, *The Zen Teaching of Jesus*, 85.
[112] Ibid, 95.
[113] Angelia Duckworth, *Grit* (New York: Scribner, 2016), 180.

we drive expecting some disconcerting jolts and that makes them far less disconcerting.

On a bulletin board out in front of a church, these lines brought out my pen and notebook: "Don't ask God to make it easy. He may be trying to stretch your faith." Where else is faith going to be stretched? Where else are we going for some toughening-up exercises? Where else are we going to learn the lessons that we will need at some future date? Making it easy will never develop our spiritual muscles; being a spiritual couch potato will only make us weaker.

> When you consider the hardships of life – the disappointments, hurts, losses, illnesses, all the tragedies you may suffer – and shift your perception to see them as opportunities for learning and growth, you become empowered…To ease this process of learning, you must master the basic lessons of compassion, forgiveness, ethics, and, ultimately, humor.[114]

Of course, this is not an easy decision to make and it is never a once and for all time decision. We have to make it a daily determination in our lives. The key in the above quote is that the hardships of life only *offer opportunities* for learning and growth. Appropriating them for such outcomes requires a belief that nothing we encounter in life should ever be wasted; whatever comes our way can be used for something constructive, be it ever so small or difficult to achieve.

In Shakespeare's *As You Like It*, we have the now memorable suggestion: "Sweet are the uses of adversity." Marilynne Robinson uses a word I think I prefer and makes these comments:

> "*Strange* are the uses of adversity." That's a fact. When I'm up here in my study with the radio on and some old book in my hands and it's night-time and the wind blows and the house creaks, I forget where I am, and it's as though I'm back in hard times for a minute or two, and there's a sweetness in the experience which I don't understand. But that only enhances

---

114 Cherie Carter-Scott, *If Life is a Game…These Are the Rules* (Naperville, IL: Simple Truths, 1998), 44.

the value of it. My point here is that you never do know the actual nature of even your own experience.[115]

It is when I look back on my times of adversity that there is mixture of strangeness and sweetness I gain from those experiences. I had no idea at the time what benefits would be mine from an experience that appeared only devastating. Whoever said, "We live life forward, but only understand it backward," was right. Perhaps a major reason for that was voiced by Oliver Hardy (of the famous Laurel and Hardy comedies): "Life is not confused, if you know how. But it is muddled."[116] Perhaps in times of adversity life is so muddled that we are unable to know the actual nature of our own experience.

QUOTES WORTH THINKING ABOUT

> If God as Maker and Ruler were in charge of it all, then why would there be so much cruelty, disaster, and death? Where is the Good in all this? The statement of the problem of evil goes back, according to David Hume, all the way to Epicurus (341-270 BCE): An all-powerful, all-knowing, and morally perfect God would prevent evil. Evil exists. Therefore, God does not. Traditional theodicies, or justifications of God, seek either to show that an omnipotent God is somehow compatible with the existence of evil or that evil, per se, does not truly exist in God's world. Emmanuel Levinas calls this out as blasphemy. The sacred exists in human life through the *acknowledgment of the incomprehensibility of evil.*[117]

From the TV-comedy *Sanford and Son* comes this kicker line: "This is the big one, Elizabeth!" Here is the stumbling block of all stumbling blocks for many who have experienced some of the most shocking cruelties in history. In the face of the Holocaust (the Shoah), any explanations or justification for God's silence and

---

115 Marilynne Robinson, *Gilead,* 108-109.
116 Paul Johnson, *Humorists* (New York: HarperCollins, 2010), 160.
117 Peter J. Brown, *Listening for God* (Macon: Mercer University Press, 2020), 230.

absence, turn to dust in our mouths. I have read much about its horror and still cannot imagine evil of such magnitude. One of those reads is *The Sunflower* by Simon Wisenthal in which he writes:

> On the day of the selection in May 1944 when the last two hundred eighty children remaining the camp were deported to Auschwitz together with the old people and the sick, my cousin (a very observant Jew) said: "I don't believe in God anymore." Till the day he died he never regained his faith.[118]

What could possibly be said to that cousin to explain what happened? I ask myself, "How would I have felt if I had experienced what happened in that Nazi concentration camp? What would have been my reply to Wisenthal's cousin?" Cynthia Ozick calls Arthur Cohen's *The Tremendum* "*a precarious, trembling, daring, prodigious book on the God-condition after the Holocaust.*"[119] David Tracy, who provides that quote, then says, "All traditional theodicies, Jewish and Christian, as well as all traditional secular anthropodicies collapse in the face of the Shoah."[120] Here is the closest Tracy comes to a "solution" of the "God condition" after the Holocaust:

> Many mystics, both Buddhist and monotheistic, refuse to ask the reason for many horrors that infest our lives. Hence Meister Eckhart's "Learn to live without a why."[121]

COMING TO SOME CONCLUSIONS

We should never forget that the great scandal of the early church should be the scandal of the modern church. In order to appeal to today's culture, some churches have removed religious symbols from their meeting places. I am told it is in order to look as little like church as possible. Wonder what Paul would think of this in light of his words to the church at Corinth: *For I decided to*

---
118 Simon Wisenthal, *The Sunflower* (New York: Shocken Books, 1998), 122.
119 David Tracy, *Filaments*, 310.
120 Ibid.
121 Ibid, 73.

know nothing among you except Jesus Christ, and him crucified? The cross appears not only to have been a stumbling block to many in Paul's day but appears to remain so to many today:

> *While Judeans ask for miraculous signs, and Greeks study philosophy, we are proclaiming Christ crucified – to the Judeans an obstacle, to the gentiles mere folly, but to those who have received the call, whether Judeans or Greeks, Christ, the power of God and the wisdom of God* (1 Corinthians 1:22-24, TAUSSIG).

The Palm Sunday crowd was looking for a Messiah who would overthrow the power of Rome and reestablish Israel as an independent nation. Their cry of "Hosannah!" meant: "Save us now!" Neither Jewish theology or the gentile world's philosophy could imagine a crucified king. Besides, the cross speaks of things we'd rather not think about – agony, suffering, pain, death. That is why many jump from Palm Sunday to Easter Sunday; it is so much easier. Liturgically, the Sunday before Easter is designated "Passion Sunday" and is the beginning of a Holy Week that includes Maundy Thursday, Black Friday, and Holy Saturday.

> In all accounts, the Risen Body still carries Christ's scars and reveals them too – hands, feet, and side are all mentioned. Remember the resurrection is not woundedness denied, forgotten, or even totally healed. It is always *woundedness transformed.*[122]

The cross has forever transformed the wounds that life inflicts upon us because, not only has Christ suffered for us, he has suffered with us. No religion at any time or place in the world has ever conceived of a crucified God. Even the disciples felt that Friday meant it was all over; they had no idea it was just the beginning. This is not so much another theodicy as it is another demonstration of God's incomprehensibility. When we talk about the cross, the first word we come up with is incomprehensibility. When we talk about resurrection, the first word we come up with is incom-

---

122 Richard Rohr, *Immortal Diamond*, 161-162.

prehensibility. Our conclusion is thus: Thank you, God, for your incomprehensibility!

Questions for Reflection and Conversation

1. Do you believe that difficulties and tragedies are a part of life?
2. In your life, where have you discovered hardships as an opportunity for Learning and growth?
3. How do you respond to the idea that "the sacred exists in human life through the acknowledgment of the incomprehensibility of evil"?

11

Faith Always Comes In A Step Behind Love

Biblical Perspectives

Galatians 5:6:
The only thing that counts is faith working through love.

Faith, working through love, is everything (TUSSIG).

What matters is faith that makes its power felt through love (JB).

Matthew 22:36-40:
"Teacher, which commandment in the law is the greatest?" He said to him, "'You shall love the Lord your God with all your heart, and with all your soul, and with all your mind.' This is the greatest and first commandment. And a second is like it: 'You shall love your neighbor as yourself.' On these two commandments hang all the law and the prophets."

"Teacher, which is the supreme commandment in the Law?" He said to him, "'You are to love the Lord your God with all your heart, and with all you soul, and with all your capacity.' This is the first and foremost commandment. There is a second that matches it. 'You are to love your neighbour as yourself.' On these two commandments hinge the entire Law and the Prophets" (SCHONFIELD).

However you translate these two texts, they come out the same: the great priority in the Christian faith is love. It is the only thing that counts; it is everything; it is the way faith makes its power felt. Jesus' response to the question about the greatest commandment has two parts, which Schonfield translates as a matched set: the love of God and the love of others. Jesus declares that the entire Law, all 613 commandments, hang on these two commandments; they are the hinge on which all the other commandments turn. Without the priority of these two loves, all the Law comes apart at the seams.

Whenever people talk about the Ten Commandments, I remind them that there are actually Eleven Commandments in Scripture. The eleventh is found in John 13:34-35 and supplies a shocking, if mostly, ignored addendum: *"I give you a new commandment, that you love one another. Just as I have loved you, you also should love one another. By this everyone will know that you are my disciples, if you have love for one another."* The mark that will designate them as his disciples will be their love for one another. Nowhere else can I find a single characteristic that is proof Christ's followers are just that. I've always wondered what would happen if Christians decided that their biggest challenge was to out-love one another? This new commandment gives context to the kind of love called for in Matthew 22. However, there is yet another dimension to this love that gives it its final shape.

> John 3:16:
> *For God so loved the world that he gave his only Son…*

For God loved the world so dearly as to give his Only-begotten Son…(SCHONFIELD).

For God loved the world in this way: He gave His One and Only Son…(HOLMAN).

When Jesus gave his new commandment, it was on the night of what we call "The Last Supper." It was given just prior to the agony in the garden, the arrest, and the crucifixion. It demonstrated the kind of love that is willing to sacrifice everything for the sake of those loved. It was the kind of love that was willing to pay any price for forgiveness, reconciliation, and redemption. It was the kind of love that caused God to send his son into the world. It was the kind of love that came in the shape of a cross.

On the table of "bargain religion," in addition to cheap grace and cheap faith, you will also find cheap love. It is another "no cost" item which is equal in its benefits to "no cost grace" and "no cost faith." It is a love built more on emotion than commitment. It is a fair-weather love that doesn't have much to sustain it when life's storms come crashing in. It is a love that doesn't make much room for inconvenience, disappointment, or sacrifice. It doesn't come close to the agape love that fills the pages of the New Testament.

Nowhere has genuine love been better described than in 1 Corinthians 13:4-8. What is most important to note is that this description is written in verbs, not adjectives. Love is demonstrated by what it does, not by how it feels. Love manifests itself by action and is not controlled by our emotions. This love is tough stuff. It is God's great gift to us and, of course, our great gift to those around us. Here are two excellent descriptions of what love does:

> *Love is long-suffering, and kind; love is never envious, never boastful, never conceited, never behaves unbecomingly; love is never self-seeking, never provoked, never reckons up her wrongs; love never rejoices at evil, but rejoices in the triumph of truth; love bears with all things, ever trustful, ever hopeful, ever patient. Love never fails* (TAUSSIG).
>
> *The love of which I speak is slow to lose patience – it looks for a way of being constructive. It is not possessive: it is neither anxious to impress nor does it cherish inflated ideas of its own importance. Love has good manners and does not pursue selfish advantage. It is not touchy. It does not keep account of evil or gloat over the wickedness of other people. On the contrary, it is glad with all good men (sic) when truth prevails. Love knows no limit to its endurance, no end to its trust, no fading of its hope; it can outlast anything. It is, in fact, the one thing that still stands when all else has fallen* (PHILLIPS).

It is no wonder that of the three things which endure – faith, hope, and love – the greatest of them is love. This kind of love. The love that changes everything. The love that changes everyone. The love with which God's son entered the world. The love that is to indicate those who are truly Jesus' disciples.

Exploring and Considering

> When the various difficulties of making our film about Mother Teresa and the Missionaries of Charity had all been dealt with, and we were in a position to go ahead, Mother Teresa said to me: "Now let us do something beautiful for God." I found the phrase enchanting, with a sparkle of gaiety very characteristic of her. It continued to echo in my mind, and when the time came to choose a title for the film, *Something Beautiful for God* seemed the obvious one. Likewise for the book.[123]

In the ugliness and squalor of Calcutta, both the film and the book are descriptions of many beautiful things for God. That's the difference love makes; it doesn't need beautiful conditions in order to do beautiful things. Love is transforming in its power to reshape and redeem in the midst of hopelessness. Of course, it is never simple or easy; it is always costly. But that cost is always worth paying because of the dividends – many of which are eternal.

For years I missed the most important aspect of an act of love and devotion given by both Mark and Matthew. Mark sets the scene at Bethany, just before Passover, shortly before the crucifixion. An unnamed woman anoints the head of Jesus with a very expensive ointment. Some present object to such a waste but Jesus defends her by saying (in the KVJ on which I was raised): *"She hath wrought a good work on me."* By far, the better translation is: *"She has done a beautiful thing to me"* (TNIV). When a good deed becomes a beautiful deed, we are thrown into another dimension

---

123 Malcolm Muggeridge, *Something Beautiful for God,* 125.

of reality; there is a transcendence about it that defies the logic of what was done.

In his later work Bernard Lonergan formulated an understanding of faith as "a new knowledge born of love" in *Method of Theology*. Lonergan also wrote a book on a new theory of economics, which has been praised by several economists but which I am not competent to judge.[124]

If you have read David Tracy, you know he is no lightweight. His writings provide territory for heavy plowing and his modest claim in the above quote is a reminder that even the best have their limits of expertise. But it doesn't take a genius to begin to understand faith as "a new knowledge born of love." I think it was Mark Twain who said: "It's not the parts of the Bible I don't understand that trouble me; it's the part's I do understand that give me the most trouble." Jesus' teaching on love, Paul's description of love, and the many passages in Scripture that call for our love for God and our love for one another are all too clear. Deep down we know this is how we are meant to live. All that remains is to put it into practice.

Quotes Worth Thining About

Sara Miles: "I don't know if I'll ever be capable of loving my enemies; I'm not always capable of forgiving myself."[125]

Being assured that we are loved and forgiven is one thing; feeling we are loved and forgiven is another thing. I am reading a new book on Martin Luther and the Reformation and reminded that he had the same problem. After confession following confession and acts of penance, he still did not feel forgiven. I really believe his breakthrough came with faith as a new knowledge born of love. For many of us, forgiving ourselves is a long process of allowing ourselves to feel loved and accepted by God as we are. Just as we are, before we do anything to get ourselves cleaned up. God's love

---

124 David Tracy, *Filaments*, 191.
125 Sara Miles, *Take This Bread*, 51.

really is the 1 Corinthian 13 love to the unlimited extreme. Jesus never met a person who was outside the circle of God's love. Jesus never met a person who was ineligible for an invitation to the Lord's Table. God's love and grace just keep on coming: *Though sin is shown to be wide and deep, thank God his grace is wider and deeper still!* (Romans 5:20, PHILLIPS).

> Unconditional love means that we don't love on the condition that we understand.[126]

That applies to friends as well as enemies. (Note: we love our enemies, not through certain emotions, but by the actions described in 1 Corinthians 13). When people complain that they don't understand someone, I sometimes respond with, "That's nothing. I don't understand myself." If love is based on understanding, it is going to be almost non-existent. We all cry out for unconditional love; if it is conditional, it isn't love, it is based on something we do to merit that love. Love that is earned isn't love and can disappear in the blink of an eye. The beginning of our love for others comes as we begin to comprehend God's unconditional love for us. "If only" has no place in the vocabulary of genuine love. If you meet someone who has an "if only" love, it will not be long until you discover a "no longer" love. Conditional love has no staying power. After all, it's when we're "down and out," when we're not at our best, that we need the lift and encouragement of unconditional love.

Coming to Some Conclusions

> (In speaking about the Trinity): God is a verb more than a noun. God is love, which means relationship itself (I John 4:7-8).[127]

"As the Father has loved me, so have I loved you" (TNIV). These are Jesus' words just prior to giving his new commandment about the disciples loving one another. Although no one has ever

---

126 Thomas Moore, *Original Self,* 74.
127 Richard Rohr, *Immortal Diamond,* 98.

Faith Never Stands Alone

explained to my satisfaction the mystery of the Trinity, many have written about how it demonstrates a relationship of love within the very nature of God. Scripture bears witness to the revelation of God as Father, Son, and Holy Spirit but never explains exactly how all these three come together as One. Jesus speaks of the Father's love for him and of his love for the Father. The all-night prayer sessions spoken of in the Gospels, must have had large segments devoted to Jesus opening his life to the love of the Father, of his being loved, and of his feeling loved.

I can think of no better conclusion to this section than these verses from I John 4:

I John 4:7-8, 10-11, 16, 19, 21:

> *Dear friends, let us love one another, for love comes from God. Everyone who loves has been born of God and knows God. Whoever does not love does not know God.*
>
> *This is love: not that we loved God, but that he loved us and sent his Son as an atoning sacrifice for our sins. Dear friends, since God so loved us, we also ought to love one another.*
>
> *God is love.*
>
> *We love because he first loved us.*
>
> *And he has given us this command: Those who love God must also love one another.*

QUESTIONS FOR REFLECTION AND CONVERSATION

1. Do you agree that the great priority in the Christian faith is love?
2. Are you surprised that 1 Corinthians 13 describes love in verbs?
3. Do you think understanding must come before love?

12

Faith and Doubt Belong Together

Biblical Perspectives

> *Jesus immediately reached out his hand and caught him, saying to him, "You of little faith, why did you doubt?"* (Matthew 14:31).

> *Then Elijah became afraid and immediately ran for his life. When he came to Beersheba that belonged to Judah, he left his servant there, but he went on a day's journey into the wilderness. He sat down under a broom tree and prayed that he might die. He said, "I have had enough! Lord, take my life, for I'm no better than my fathers." Then he lay down and slept under the broom tree.* (1 Kings 19:3-5; HOLMAN).

> *Cursed be the day*
> *on which I was born.*
> *The day my mother bore me –*
> *let it never be blessed.*
> *Cursed be the man*
> *who brought the news to my father, saying,*
> *"A male child is born to you,"*
> *bringing you great joy.*
> *...*
> *Why did I come out of the womb*
> *to see (only) struggle and sorrow,*
> *to end my life in shame?*
> (Jeremiah 20:14-15, 18), HOLMAN).

After a day of teaching that concluded with the miraculous feeding of five thousand, Jesus instructed his disciples to take the boats to the other side of the sea while he went up on the mountain to pray. Sometime between three and six in the morning, with the wind whipping up choppy waters, suddenly Jesus appears walking on the water (Matthew 14:22-33). The disciples are terrified but Jesus calms them with, *"Take heart, it is I. Do not be afraid."* Peter is the only one to speak: *"If it is you, command me to come to you on the water."* The invitation is extended, Peter gets out of the boat, is alarmed by the strong wind, and, beginning to sink, cries out to be saved. Jesus extends his saving hand and then chastises him for his doubt.

Impulsive Peter is true to form and quickly discovers that his courage (faith) is not sufficient in the face of Galilee's fierce winds and churning waves. Many sermons have spoken to Jesus' calming presence in the storms of life and of the need for faith when life is at its most dangerous. The reality is, Peter should never have gotten out of the boat; Jesus did not call him to "test" his faith. His was a foolish gesture of braggadocio in front of the other disciples. It is a prelude to his later, *"Even if all the others deny you, I will remain faithful"* (Matthew 26:33). Of course, he doesn't. Some see this incident as Jesus' mastery over the power of the sea, the anti-creation chaos monster.[128] A key verse in this section is Matthew 14:33: *And those in the boat worshiped him, saying, "Truly you are the Son of God."* The other key verse is 14:27: *"Take heart, it is I; do not be afraid."* This parallels Jesus' resurrection saying in Matthew 28:10: *"Do not be afraid."*

Here, in the texts that open this chapter, is one of the pillars of the early church and two of the greatest prophets, being overcome with doubt and fear (being the opposite of faith). As much as we would like to have examples of how to live a life of faith free of doubt, faith and doubt appear to belong together. Peter seems to be in danger of drowning, Elijah is fleeing from Jezebel who

---

[128] *The New Interpreter's Bible,* Volume VIII (Nashville: Abingdon Press, 1995), 328.

has threated to kill him, and Jeremiah is in total despair over the apparent failure of his mission as God's prophet and the resulting mockery and persecution. These are but three examples of great people of faith who are not one-hundred-percenters. For most of us (I speak for myself), this is not achievable. Faith has nothing to do with perfection (more about this in Chapter 16).

EXPLORING AND CONSIDERING

> *"If you are able to do anything, have pity on us and help us." Jesus said to him, "If you are able! – All things can be done for the one who believes." Immediately the father of the child cried out, "I believe; help my unbelief!"* (Mark 9:22-24).

The father who brings his epileptic son (modern diagnosis) to Jesus, appears not fully convinced of Jesus' ability to heal him. (You wonder how many other "healers" he has tried.) Jesus' immediate rebuke is startling in its dimensions: *"All things can be done for the one who believes."* When the father confesses his mixture of belief and unbelief, Jesus responds by healing his son. Jesus responds to faith mixed with doubt. Less than a full faith is sufficient. All the father can do is exercise the faith he does have; it proves to be enough. In spite of remaining unbelief, his faith provides enough of a foundation for Jesus to work his healing. In some places there was so much unbelief that what Jesus could do was limited (Matthew 13:58). A philosophy that sounds strange may come from this episode: Exercise whatever faith you have and don't worry about the fragments of unbelief.

> Frederick Buechner in *Listening to Your Life: If there were no room for doubt, there would be no room for me.*[129]

I'm glad the church has always made room for those of us who have faith but continue to struggle with doubt. This doubt usually surfaces as we deal with the suffering and tragedies in life that defy logic or any religious justification (e.g. the Holocaust). Prayers are

---
129 Frederick Buechner, *Listening to Your Life*, 91.

not always answered and good does not always triumph over evil. Things do not always turnout okay. There is not always light at the end of the tunnel, sometimes it is just another tunnel. Sometimes it helps to put this into perspective on the lighter side of things, like this from the novel *Miss Julia Speaks Her Mind:*[130]

> It's funny about women and children, isn't it! There was Hazel Marie Puckett, with no money, no home, and no husband. Yet she had a child. And here I was, a respectable married woman with everything to give to a child, and the Lord hadn't seen fit. This was just one more situation where I wondered what in the world He was thinking of.

You don't have to live very long until you agree with Wendell Berry: "The mind that is not baffled is not employed!" Richard Rohr adds his comment to the quote: "The major spiritual problem for many religious people is that they refused to be baffled for a while."[131] A realistic assessment of so many things that happen in the world can only be classified as "baffling." They defy explanation and I am particularly weary of those who try to provide them for the inexplicable in life. Even Jesus refused to explain the baffling. When his disciples ask why a man was born blind (John 9:1f), Jesus doesn't default to the usual reason of sin. His explanation goes no further than *"Neither this man or his parents sinned."* His response is his solution to the problem: *"I will use the occasion of his blindness to demonstrate the grace of God"* (my interpretation). He then heals the blind man – but the baffling issue of being born blind remains. I do think it is interesting that Jesus never asks the blind man about his faith.

Here is the classic example of one whose works of faith were astounding while her bouts with doubt were almost crippling:

> After her death, Mother Teresa's private papers revealed that she had suffered from incredible doubt, and for long peri-

---

130 Ann B. Ross, *Miss Julia Speaks Her Mind* (New York: William Morrow, 1999), 128.
131 Richard Rohr, *Immortal Diamond*, 138.

ods of her life she felt that God was absent. Using words like "darkness," "dryness," "torture," and "loneliness," she wrote about the spiritual agony she often experienced, comparing it to hell and revealing that at one time her doubts were so great that she even questioned the existence of God.[132]

To say the least, many found these revelations shocking. Those who worked with her never suspected what was going on in her soul. She was always pleasant, cheerful, and never without a smile. She continued her work among the sick and dying in the streets of Calcutta. She loved those nobody else would love. She cared for those nobody else would care for. She touched those nobody else would touch. She remained faithful to the calling that was hers, even with unrelenting doubt dogging at her heels.

> Interior darkness is nothing new in the tradition of Catholic mysticism. In fact, it has been a common phenomenon among the numerous saints throughout Church history who have experienced what the Spanish Carmelite mystic St. John of the Cross termed the "dark night."[133]

Even the great mystics and saints have confessed: Faith and doubt belong together.

QUOTES WORTH THINKING ABOUT

> Martin Luther's concept of the Hidden and Revealed God is Luther's singular contribution to all Christian theological understanding of God.[134]

We do know some things about God because of the revelation In Jesus Christ and the witness of Holy Scripture. Not everything is hidden but not everything is revealed. We know enough to be able to trust him and begin our journey of faith. As Paul confesses,

---

132 Matthew Kelly, *Rediscover the Saints* (North Palm Beach: Blue Sparrow, 2019), 75.
133 Mother Teresa, *Come Be My Light*, 22.
134 David Tracy, *Filaments*, 141.

we are still *those looking at puzzling reflections in a mirror* (1 Corinthians 13:12, PHILLIPS). The polished metal mirrors of his day did not give the clear images of our present-day mirrors. "Puzzling reflections" indicates how much remains hidden in the reflection. If we are seeking full disclosure from God that will enable us to have faith based on crystal clear understanding, we are destined to be disappointed.

> The English romantic poet John Keats wrote to his brother in 1817 that to be a person of achievement, one must have "negative capability," which he described as "capable of being in uncertainties, mysteries, doubts, without any irritable reaching after fact and reason."[135]

If we are waiting for all the facts or for a catalogue of reasons for what happens in life, we will only find irritation for ourselves and for those around us. Faith is what enables us to live with the uncertainties, mysteries, and doubts that are all a part of what has rightly been termed the "human dilemma." The courage to continue in faith and hope, regardless of inexplicable circumstances, is what real faith is all about. Mother Teresa illustrates this kind of faith. If everything is certain, everything is clearly explained, and there is not a doubt in your mind, why would you need faith?

> No reading of any great classic can ever prove definitive. Classic texts are at best fragmentary.[136]

David Tracy makes a strong case for the impossibility of drafting full and final positions on almost anything. He argues that the best we can do is to offer fragments and filaments. It seems to me this is Paul's confession in 1 Corinthians 13:12 – *Now I know only in part...* The difficulty in maintaining faith, is that it has to be built on parts, on fragments. In this life, we will never have a full, final, finished story that is complete down to the last detail with the byline: nothing more need be said. In this life, there is always

---

135 Kate Murphy, *You're Not Listening* (New York: Celadon Books, 2019), 87.
136 David Tracy, *Filaments*, 74.

more to be said. I believe that will probably hold true for the next life as well.

It might be good to end this section on a lighter note from a novel:

> I decided to be very un-Sam-like (her name) and not worry about it, although I worked around that by spending the time I'd saved by not worrying in worrying that not worrying was really a worrying sign.[137]

As with so many things in this human pilgrimage, we finally decide to do the best we can and not worry about the lack of perfection in any area of our lives – including faith. Worry is never an addition; it is always a subtraction. It is life's great detractor; it is life's great thief. I have always been encouraged by people like William Carey, a life-long missionary to India, and, in 1792, the founder of the English Baptist Missionary Society. He was a man of many achievements but, when asked his legacy, I remember that he replied, "I can plod. I want to be remembered as a plodder." That's probably the best that most of us can do, and there's nothing wrong with it. Plodders can accomplish a great deal concentrating on who they are, what they have, with whatever faith and courage they can muster.

COMING TO SOME CONCLUSIONS

In my years of group Bible studies, too many people identified the disciple Thomas as "Doubting Thomas," even though this designation is nowhere in the New Testament. It gets pinned on him because, when Jesus initially appears to the disciples after his resurrection, for some reason, Thomas is not with the group. When informed that they had seen the Lord, his reaction in John 20:24-25 is: "*I'll not believe until I see for myself*" (my free translation).

I do not see this so much as doubting them as needing first-hand knowledge. I have always thought of him as "honest

---

[137] Judith Flanders, A Bed of Scorpions (New York: Minotaur Books, 2016), 92.

Thomas" because of this and another episode earlier in John's Gospel. When Jesus announces his departure in John 14, he tells the disciples, *"You know the way to the place where I am going."* I don't think any of the disciples had any idea what Jesus was talking about. Only Thomas is brave enough to speak: *"Lord, we do not know where you are going. How can we know the way?"* Honest Thomas speaks up to say, "We don't understand what you are talking about."

In John 11, Jesus announces he is going back to Judea because the message has come that Lazarus is gravely ill. His disciples voice their alarm: *"Rabbi, the Jews were just now trying to stone you, and are you going there again?"* (11:8). Jesus tells them he must go because Lazarus has died. The only recorded response by any of the disciples is the one from Thomas: *"Let us also go, that we may die with him"* (11:16). Honest Thomas has courage to match his faith and commitment.

His final appearance in the John's Gospel comes a week following Jesus' initial appearance to the disciples. Jesus makes his appearance again, and invites Thomas to see his hands and touch his wounded side. *"Do not doubt, but believe,"*

(John 14:27). Thomas' response is the immediate supreme confession in the entire Gospel: *"My Lord and my God"* (John 14:28). This supposedly doubting Thomas has become the great confessing Thomas of the Gospel. He simply had to see and believe for himself; no second-hand faith was sufficient.

I have always thought it significant that the disciples made a place for Thomas a week following their encounter with Jesus, even though Thomas would not commit himself on the basis of their experience. They made a place in their fellowship for a doubter.

> A lot of people think the hardest part about religious doubt is feeling isolated from God. It's not. At least in my experience, the hardest part about doubt is feeling isolated from your community.[138]

---

138 Rachel Held Evans, *Inspired*, 68.

Faith Never Stands Alone

Rachel Held Evans reminds us that, just as the disciples made room for Thomas, the church needs to be a welcoming community for those who have honest doubts. Sunday School classes only become places of learning if those who attend feel comfortable in a free and open discussion where judgment is not on the table. Honest Thomas is remembered for his courage and his confession of faith. The doubting did not mean exclusion but inclusion until he moved beyond his doubt.

Big sidebar: Even if you are never able to move beyond your doubts (like Mother Teresa), the church needs to be a place of equal participation and fellowship. After all, faith and doubt go together.

Questions For Reflection and Conversation

1. Can you think of any biblical heroes who had "perfect" faith?
2. Do you believe it's perfectly okay to be baffled for a while?
3. What do you think about Mother Teresa's disclosure of her "incredible doubt"?

13

WRONG TURNS AND DETOURS ARE PART OF A FAITH-JOURNEY

BIBLICAL PERSPECTIVES

They went through the region of Phrygia and Galatia, having been forbidden by the Holy Spirit to speak the word in Asia. When they had come opposite Mysia, they attempted to go into Bithynia, but the Spirit of Jesus did not allow them; so passing by Mysia, they went down to Troas. During the night Paul had a vision: there stood a man of Macedonia pleading with him and saying, "Come over to Macedonia and help us." When he had seen the vision, we immediately tried to cross over to Macedonia, being convinced that God had called us to proclaim the good news to them (Acts 16:6-10).

After some days Paul said to Barnabas, "Come, let us return and visit the believers in every city where we proclaimed the word of the Lord and see how they are doing." Barnabas wanted to take with them John called Mark. But Paul decided not to take with them one who had deserted them in Pamphylia and had not accompanied them in their work. The disagreement became so sharp that they parted company; Barnabas took Mark with him and sailed away to Cyprus. But Paul chose Silas and set out, the believers' commending him to the grace of the Lord. He went through Syria and Cilicia, strengthening the churches (Acts 15:36-41).

> *When he had gone through these regions and had given the believers much encouragement, he came to Greece, where he stayed for three months. He was about to set sail for Syria when a plot was made against him by the Jews, and so he decided to return through Macedonia* (Acts 20:2-3).

The shortest distance between two points often is not the path on which we are permitted to travel. Three interruptions and alterations in Paul's planned itinerary are prominent in these three selections from Acts. Each has a distinctive context. In the first, the Holy Spirit and then the Spirit of Jesus reject the initial plans Paul makes. In the second, an unreasonable conflict necessitates a change in traveling companions. In the third, a potentially dangerous situation calls for a re-routing. We will briefly see how each of these applies to avoiding wrong turns or forced to make detours.

We are not told how the Holy Spirit or the Spirit of Jesus communicated to Paul the need to cancel his intended trips. "The heightening of terminology in vv. 6—10 from 'the Holy Spirit,' to 'the Spirit of Jesus,' to 'God' is not just stylistic but an unconscious expression of the early church's embryonic trinitarian faith."[139] The new destination is revealed in a "vision." Dreams and visions were accepted ways in which God revealed his will and purpose. We do not have a recorded word from Joseph (Mary's betrothed), but four times (Matthew 1:20; 2:13; 2:19; 2:22) we are told he responds to dreams that provide directions. Paying attention to our dreams is a positive and biblical practice.

John Mark, Barnabas's cousin, becomes the source of an unresolved quarrel that results in Paul's choosing Silas as his traveling companion. Paul must have been deeply wounded by Mark's earlier desertion and is not prepared to have this "quitter" rejoin them. He was honest about his inability to work with John Mark. Personality conflicts cannot always be resolved, going separate ways may be the only solution. Disagreements between two such prominent missionaries as Paul and Barnabas are sad but instructive, in that they let us know that, from the beginning, even the church leaders

---

139 *The Expositor's Bible* (Grand Rapids: Zondervan, 1981), 457.

were human beings. What seems important to me is that Paul's ministry did not cease because of this conflict, but, in one sense, was doubled.

The third change in plans resulted from an obvious danger:

> At the end of three months in Corinth, Paul sought to sail for Palestine-Syria, doubtless intending to reach Jerusalem in time for the great pilgrim festival of Passover and probably on a Jewish pilgrim ship. But a plot to kill him at sea was uncovered, and he decided to travel overland through Macedonia.[140]

Sometimes, a hazard in the prospective journey is discovered and a change in routing is absolutely necessary. Paul must have had friends who kept him posted about potential dangers to his personal safety. Safety is not always the only concern but taking foolish risks is not a good travel plan. Paul doesn't need a vision, dream, or divine directive to know when a sea voyage should be cancelled. The obvious should always be in our sights so that we can make intelligent decisions. Following God's purpose and plans for our lives doesn't mean we put our minds in storage.

Exploring and Considering

"Road Work Ahead: Expect Delays." This is the sign we ought to post somewhere easily visible when we are beginning our plans for the day. There is always something that needs a little repair work and there is always something that makes whatever we are doing take longer than expected. It is not something in life designed to frustrate us, it is just the nature of life, even the life of faith.

> But be warned. In Scripture, and in life, the road to deliverance nearly always takes a detour. Rarely do the people of God reach any kind of promised land without a journey or two through the wilderness.[141]

---

140 Ibid, 507.
141 Rachel Held Evans, *Inspired*, 48.

Those who celebrated their release from bondage in Egypt never envisioned a wilderness (desert) in their future. It was supposed to be a direct journey to a land flowing with milk and honey. We should all expect wilderness experiences to be part of any journey to any destination. If we are not careful, we will allow ourselves to become just as frustrated and discouraged as the group that had Moses as their guide. There is also plenty of evidence that, on more than one occasion, Moses joined them in their frustration.

When people remind me that "It's always something," I occasionally disagree by responding, "No, sometimes it's several things at once." That's just the nature of wilderness travel - it's the land of multiple issues. That's why an important ingredient in our faith should be flexibility.

> This book (*Think Again*) is an invitation to let go of knowledge and opinions that are no longing serving you well, and anchor your sense of self in flexibility rather than consistency...A hallmark of wisdom is knowing when it is time to abandon some of your most reassured tools – and some of the most cherished parts of your identity.[142]

If our travel through life is all on a four-lane interstate, it might be possible to set the cruise control and just relax. Instead, we are called to adjust to changing conditions and circumstances that come as we move through life. We have to live the self-examined life on a daily basis and know what things (and ideas) will not serve us in our present situation. I cannot resist another short quip from *Think Again*:

> The accelerating pace of change means that we need to question our beliefs more readily than ever before. This is not an easy task. As we sit with our beliefs, they tend to become more extreme and more entrenched. *I'm still struggling to accept that Pluto is not a planet.*[143]

---

142 Adam Grant, *Think Again*, 12.
143 Ibid, 17.

Faith Never Stands Alone

For most of us, the beliefs that need to be questioned are not necessarily about our faith but about life. Why do we believe all the things we do about nearly every aspect of life? We were not born with any of these beliefs. We have acquired them along the way. We need to examine where they came from and if they are serving us or enslaving us. Flexibility means that we are willing to listen carefully to how we are being challenged and determine what changes we need to make in order best to go forward. Israel discovered that living in the wilderness called for an entirely different playbook than living in Egypt. It sometimes takes great wisdom to realize, "We're not in Kansas anymore." When we find ourselves in Dorothy's OZ, it takes flexibility in just about everything. We need to be adaptable in order to be our best and do our best whatever our faith-journey offers.

QUOTES WORTH THINKING ABOUT

> Focusing on results might be good for short-term performance, but can be an obstacle to long-term learning...Along with outcome accountability, we can create process accountability....[144]

Even if we focus on the result of our travel, in the process of going, we are determining the quality of the experience of our destination. A "bad trip" can derail a great deal of the pleasure that is expected at the destination. It is while we are "on the way," that learning opportunities not available at the end, are possible. My rule for most of what we do in life is simple: if the process is viewed as something to get through as quickly as possible, the result almost always falls short of expectations. Since most of life is process, we should give at least equal time to process accountability as we do to outcome accountability.

> It has become a cliché to talk about faith as a journey, and yet the metaphor holds. Scripture doesn't speak of people

---

[144] Ibid, 217.

who *found* God. Scripture speaks of people who *walked* with God. This is a keep-moving, one foot-in-front-of-the-other, who-knows-what's-next-deal, and you never exactly arrive.[145]

From the very beginning of the biblical narrative, we have the picture of God seeking us: God comes walking in the Garden seeking Adam and Eve who have gone into hiding; God breaks into Abram's life by calling him to begin a journey to a distant, unknown land; on an ordinary day of shepherding, Moses' life is changed by the theophany of a burning bush; and Paul is overcome by the light and voice of the one he has been violently opposing. In all these cases, it is God who takes the initiative, it is God who is the seeker. The great paradox is that each of these had to allow themselves to be found. With each of us, the response to grace must finally be a "yes" in order to complete the process of being found.

The one and only invitation I can find that Jesus ever gave is: *"Follow me"* (Matthew 4:19, 8:22, 9:9, 16:24, 19:21; Mark 2:14; Luke 5:27, 9:59, 18:22; John 1:43, 10:27, 12:26, 21:22). An early designation for Christians was "Followers of the Way." His followers were those "Walking the Walk." I agree with Rachel Held Evans that the most important ingredient in this walking is to keep moving,[146] even if we take wrong turns or find ourselves on a detour. Wrong turns can be corrected by getting back to the right path and detours are usually just temporary side tracks. None of the great heroes of faith we mentioned – Abraham, Moses, Paul – had any idea what was going to be in their journey or how many surprises were in store for them. They learned as they went; they discovered as they traveled. So it is with each of us. In one sense, we are all like Abraham who *set out, not knowing where he was going* (Hebrews 11:8). He let God take care of the destination, and so must we all. Our duty is to take the next obvious step in our journey.

As Homer tells the story, Odysseus mastered countless challenges during his twenty-year saga…Always, though,

---

145 Rachel Held Evans, *Searching for Sunday,* 180.
146 Ibid.

he kept going. He kept moving forward. The mantra of the quester is to keep moving forward. Whatever it takes, whether facing an immense challenge or spirit-sapping tedium, just keep making progress.[147]

Coming to Some Conclusions

A personal confession: the shortest distance between two points may be a straight line, but the best way to travel the distance between where we are and where God wants us to be probably has a lot of twists and turns in it. You are never quite certain what is around the next bend in the road or what surprises await you at a yet to be encountered intersection. My advice: let life unfold; it will whether or not we give it our permission.

In a novel, I found myself described in this observation: "He had a guilt-ridden feeling of excitement about a new assignment outside of his normal duties. He knew he was always at his best – and sometimes his worst – when he was forced out of his district and his comfort zone."[148] When I find myself in unfamiliar territory with yet to be discovered ground rules, I can easily go either way. Being at my best requires new eyes and ears to fully understand what is required in the new situation and my willingness to think differently and do differently. My confession is probably the same as yours: it is in places outside my comfort zone that I have learned the most and grown the most, but not without some missteps along the way.

Psalm 40:5 has been one of my favorite texts during those times when I wasn't quite sure what to do next: *How many plans you have made for us; you have no equal!* (JB). God always has something in mind for us. There is always another step to take. There is always a direction in which to go. Who cares if there are wrong turns and detours ahead? There is always God's sustaining love in every wrong turn, his abundant grace in every detour, and his faithfulness for

---

147 Chris Guillebeau, *The Happiness Pursuit,* 149.
148 C. J. Box, *Off the Grid* (New York: G. P. Putnam's Sons, 2016), 101.

every step (and misstep) of our journey. The words of the old gospel song ring true: *He leadeth me! O blessed thought!* That's all I need to know to keep going.

Questions For Reflection and Conversation

1. How have wrong turns and detours led to discoveries and growth In your life?
2. Do we, like the children of Israel, never expect a wilderness in our journey?
3. What is the advantage of focusing on "process accountability"?

14

What Kind Of Mountains Are Moved By Faith?

Biblical Perspectives

> *Then he entered Jerusalem and went into the temple; and when he had looked around at everything, as it was already late, he went out to Bethany with the twelve.*
>
> *Seeing in the distance a fig tree in leaf, he went to see whether perhaps he would find anything on it. When he came to it, he found nothing but leaves, for it was not the season for figs.*
>
> *Then they came to Jerusalem. And he entered the temple and began to drive out those who were selling and those who were buying in the temple, and he overturned the tables of the money changers and the seats of those who sold doves; and he would not allow anyone to carrying anything through the temple. He was teaching and saying, "Is it not written, 'My house shall be called a house of prayer for all the nations?' But you have made it a den of robbers."*
>
> *In the morning as they passed by, they saw the fig tree withered away to its roots. Then Peter remembered and said to him, "Rabbi, look! The fig tree that you cursed has withered." Jesus answered them, "Have faith in God. Truly I tell you, if you say to this mountain, 'Be taken up and thrown into the sea,' and if you do not doubt in your heart, but believe that what you say will come to pass, it will be done for you. So, I tell you, whatever you*

ask for in prayer, believe that you have received it, and it will be yours." (Mark 11:11, 13, 15-17, 20-24).

Following what is called "The Triumphal Entry" into Jerusalem, Mark relates several events related to this episode. Jesus curses a fig tree, he "cleanses" the temple, his disciples comment on the withered fig tree, Jesus talks about mountain-moving faith. Remember: the original text had no divisions into chapters and verses. Those who first heard it (most could not read), heard something quite different than most of us who read the Scripture in snippets. The whole is indeed much more than the assemblage of its parts. The context of Jesus' comment on prayer that moves mountains is both significant and alarming. How are all these events tied together?

I am in agreement with most commentators: Just as the fig tree failed in its purpose to produce fruit, so the temple's failure to fulfill its original purpose will result in its demise. (This was written before the Roman destruction of the temple in 70 CE.) "The Temple was the center of commerce for all Judea, its chief financial institution and largest bank. Judea was, for all intents and purposes, a temple-state."[149] Most of those associated with on-going operations were quite wealthy. Commerce and profit were the name of the game. The selling and money-exchanging facilities were located in the Court of the Gentiles, the only place non-Jews could gather. This court was also used as a convenient cut-through for those wanting to get to the other side of the temple.

Jesus' entry into Jerusalem was met with cries of "Hosanna!" ("Save us now"!) from those who believed he was the anointed one and that the Kingdom of God was arriving. Their expectation was that the arrival would begin with the overthrow of Roman occupation. However, the Realm of God that arrived with the coming of Jesus was neither political or commercial. It had to do with worship in spirit and in truth (John 4:23) with no need for a daily sacrificial

---

149 Reza Aslan, *Zealot* (New York: Random House, 2013), 7.

Faith Never Stands Alone

system. It had to do with inclusion and not exclusion. It had to do with grace and not law. It had to do with love and not judgment.

> *Then the disciples came to Jesus privately and said, "Why could we not cast it out?" He said to them, "Because of your little faith. For truly I tell you, if you have faith the size of a mustard seed, you will say to this mountain, 'Move from here to there,' and it will move; and nothing will be impossible for you"* (Matthew 17:19-21).

Matthew places mountain-moving faith in the context of the disciples' failed attempt to heal an epileptic son. William Barclay provides some insight with this commentary:

> When Jesus spoke about *removing mountains,* He was using a phrase which the Jews knew well. A great teacher, who could really expound and interpret scripture, and who could explain and resolve difficulties, was regularly known as an *uprooter* or, even a *pulverizer,* of mountains. To tear up, to uproot, to pulverize mountains were all regular phrase for removing difficulties. Jesus never meant this to be taken physically and literally. What he meant was: "If you have faith enough, all difficulties can be solved, and even the hardest task can be accomplished." Faith in God is the instrument which enables (us) to remove the hills of difficulty which block (our) path.[150]

Exploring and Considering

Barclay suggests to me that the kind of praying Jesus is talking about is that focused on the roadblocks that keep faith and life from moving forward. The roadblocks that prevent our becoming the persons God wants us to be and accomplishing those things that are a part of God's plan and purpose for our lives. This is not an: "Anything you decide to pray for, go for it!" All of the promises about "answered" prayer are within a context of Kingdom people

---

150 William Barclay, *The Gospel of Matthew,* Vol. 2 (Philadelphia: Westminster Press, 1958), 184-185.

seeking to live out their roles as citizens of a new day and a new order.

We aren't always accurate in our decisions about what constitutes a mountain that needs to be moved. We forever remain those who *only know imperfectly* (1 Corinthians 13:9, SCHONFIELD). I took the following test and received a failing mark:[151]

> Compared to most people, how much do you think you know about each of the following topics – more, less, or the same?

1. Why English became the official language of the United States.
2. Why women were burned at the stake in Salem.
3. What job Walt Disney did before he drew Mickey Mouse.
4. On which spaceflight humans first laid eyes on the Great Wall of China.
5. Why eating candy effects how kids behave.

> On the questions above, if you felt you know anything at all, think again. America has no official language, suspected witches were hanged in Salem but not burned, Walt Disney didn't draw Mickey Mouse (it was the work of an animator named Ub Iwerks), you can't actually see the Great Wall of China from space, and the average effect of sugar on children's behavior is zero.

Paul prayed three times for the removal of a roadblock he termed "a thorn in the flesh" (2 Corinthians 12:7-9). God's reply to his mountain-moving prayer was, *"My grace is sufficient for you,"* or in another translation, *"My gracious favor is all you need"* (NLT). The bottom line: we must always be willing to let God have the final word, which, of course, he always does! Just a reminder of our standing in the matter of who really knows best.

There are a couple of big mountains that I know respond to faith. The first has been tagged WYSIATI.

---

151 Adam Grant, *Think Again*, 40-41.

Faith Never Stands Alone

> Jumping to conclusions on the basis of limited evidence is so important to an understanding of intuitive thinking, and comes up so often in this book, that I will use a cumbersome abbreviation for it: WYSIATI, which stands for what you see is all there is.[152]

I'm going to put a somewhat different spin on this idea and suggest that, in spiritual terms, there is so much more beyond what we see. Total reality cannot be limited to what we know with our five senses; science cannot have the last word on what is and what isn't. It can only measure what is and not what lies beyond. When Nicodemus is told by Jesus that he must be born from above (John 3), he has difficulty envisioning something beyond the physical. There really is an above and beyond, there really is more than we can see or even imagine. Quantum physics has contributed to our understanding of a world much deeper and far more complex than previous generations thought possible. When we talk about galaxies, beyond galaxies, beyond galaxies we are talking about possibility beyond possibility beyond possibility.

> Martin Luther, with riveting intensity and characteristic honesty, insisted that every aspect of theology is a desperate attempt always inadequate, always necessary, to understand some aspect of the Unfathomable Mystery of God.[153]

The place to begin is with the confession that there is the unfathomable, that mystery is a reality, and that "so much more" is the watchword of faith. Everything cannot simply be tested, analyzed, explained, and understood.

The second mountain that responds to faith is closely aligned to the first one; it is the either/or mountain:

> William Wainwright's skepticism also works in the opposite direction: he is inclined to question the demands of what we might call a "narrow rationality" that ignores faith and feel-

---

[152] Daniel Kahneman, *Thinking, Fast and Slow* (New York: Farrar, Straus and Giroux, 2011), 86.
[153] David Tracy, *Filaments*, 135.

ing...I have never been able to repress the suspicion that (as William James says) the "heart" may be "our deepest organ of communication with reality."[154]

Many have spoken of the "wisdom of the heart" which should be on equal standing with the wisdom of the mind. There is always the need for "critical thinking" and "rational discourse." These are the foundation stones for conversation and meaningful dialogue in a social media driven culture. Also necessary are "right brained contributions": creativity, emotion, and intuition. It seems so obvious: we need to use both sides (all) of our brain to be whole human beings.

Theology and spirituality need to walk hand in hand:

> Spirituality as a discipline on its own, without a relationship to rigorous theological theory, philosophy, and social science, is ever in danger of becoming free-floating sentimentality. Without strict theoretical theology and philosophy, spirituality can become all too *ad hoc* as a captive of ever-shifting attitudes of the reigning culture.
>
> Theology without spirituality is existentially too thin and too removed from the biblical, liturgical, and patristic grounding sources and from the rich resources of contemporary Christian traditions of spirituality and piety, both person and communal.[155]

As with so many things in life, it is not a matter of either/or but of both/and. We need a healthy IQ as well as a healthy EQ. We need to bring our minds and our hearts together as we try to live a well-orbed life.

Quotes Worth Thinking About

In his art as in his philosophy, G. K. Chesterton fiercely defended his right to embrace old ideas and traditional methods. To paraphrase one of his remarks, he once said that the

---

154 Gary Gutting, *What Philosophy Can Do*, 131.
155 David Tracy, *Filaments*, 3-4

progressives claimed that a thing that is valid on Tuesday cannot be valid on Thursday.[156]

Some people see mountains of difficulty in traditions and ideas that have "past" stamped on them: it is only the new and fresh that meet the claims and needs of the present. I once heard in a workshop that C. S. Lewis recommended reading two old books for every new book one reads. Old ideas do not necessarily chain us to the past, they often provide the foundation on which to build. To ignore the collected and recorded wisdom of the past, as we find recorded in the great libraries of the world, is to believe we can begin at square one in most areas of knowledge and make great achievements with only the new. "New and improved" may not necessarily be the improvement we want or need. New ideas do not necessarily set us free for living in the future, especially if their shelf-life does not last long enough to be fully tested.

> Alexandros Papaderos personally did a tremendous amount to reconstruct relationship between Crete and Germany after the horrors of the Second World War. He tells the story as a boy of finding pieces of a mirror. "I began to play with the largest piece as a toy and became fascinated by the fact that I could reflect light into dark places where the sun would never shine – in deep holes and crevices and dark closets and behind walls…As I became a man, I grew to understand that this was not just child's play, but a metaphor for what I might do with my life. Every day brought the question implied by it: What dark places will I find today in need of life, and how will I manage to reflect some into it?"[157]

When the shadows of great mountains cast doubt and fear, I believe our prayers for the courage and knowhow to reflect some light of grace, hope, and healing will always be answered. No matter how broken and shattered our meager resources, they can always be used to dispel some of the darkness. Psalm 36:9 declares: *For with*

---

156 Thomas C. Peters, *The Christian Imagination: G.K. Chesterton on the Arts* (San Francisco: Ignatius Press, 2000), 74.
157 Hal Gregersen, *Questions Are the Answers,* 269-270.

you is the fountain of life; in your light we see light. Is it too much to say that in his light, we become light? In John 8:12, we read: *Jesus spoke to them saying, "I am the light of the world. Whoever follows me will never walk in darkness but will have the light of life."* Is this not why he can tell us in Matthew 5:14, *"You are the light of the world."* In this sense, we are reflected light, the reflected light of those pieces of mirror Alexandros found as a boy. Mountain-moving faith will enable us to bring the light of God's grace and love into deep holes, crevices, dark closets, and behind walls – where the sun would never shine without our reflective lives.

> Not only did Mother Teresa bring the light of Christ to the poorest of the poor; she also met Christ in each of them.[158]

This quote comes from a book of Mother Teresa's writings titled *Come Be My Light*. Sometimes the darkness of this world, very evident in places like the slums of Calcutta, seems like a mountain that can never be moved. Mother Teresa never attempted to move that mountain of despair in Calcutta, she only went out each day to bring Christ's light into the deep holes of abandonment and isolation experienced by the nobodies of India. The miracle of her work was that in bringing the light of Christ, she also met Christ in each of them. The text for such an experience is found in Matthew 25:40 – *Just as you did it to one of the least of these…you did it to me.*

COMING TO SOME CONCLUSIONS

> "I see," said Miss Climpson. "Well, none of us can do more than our best, and it is very necessary to have Faith. That moves mountains, we are told." "Then for Heaven's sake lay in a good stock of it," said Wimsey, gloomily, "because as far as I can see, this job is like shifting the Himalayas and the Alps, with a spot of frosty Caucasus and a touch of the Rockies thrown in."[159]

---

158 Mother Teresa, *Come Be My Light*, 43.
159 Dorothy Sayers, *Strong Poison*, 137.

Many are surprised to find a mystery writer who is also a theologian. Dorothy Sayers is a master of both and *Strong Poison* is one of her best mysteries. I won't give away the plot, but Lord Peter Wimsey is confronted with an almost unscalable challenge. That is why he requests a storehouse of mountain-moving faith. Perhaps this faith cannot so much be stored, as it can be practiced on a daily basis as we face the small difficulties of life. We prepare ourselves for scaling the huge mountains of difficulty by developing strength and knowhow received from climbing the easy peaks. I don't think we are remiss in thinking of faith as a muscle that can atrophy from lack of use or can grow stronger and ready for bigger jobs by being exercised on a regular basis.

As a boy, I had no idea that one of my favorite choruses was based on a song of the Panama Canal Builders:[160]

> Got any rivers they say are uncrossable,
> God any mountains they say "can't tunnel through"?
> We specialize in the wholly impossible,
> Doing the things they say you can't do.

Our Sunday School version went like this:

> Got any rivers you think are uncrossable,
> Got any mountains you can't tunnel through?
> God specializes in things thought impossible,
> He does the things others cannot do.

If you are like me, you can recall times in your life when there were mountains that were blocking the path you knew you were supposed to take. You prayed, and, because God does specialize in things thought impossible, he either moved the mountain or made a way for you to tunnel through. I remember times like that. I don't know what we would do if we did not have a God who does things others cannot do.

---

[160] L. B. Cowman, *Streams in the Desert* (Grand Rapids: Zondervan, 1997), 73.

Questions For Reflection and Conversation

1. Can you recall any mountains that were moved because of your faith?
2. What do you think about Barclay's interpretation of "removing mountains"?
3. Do you agree that we need both a healthy IQ and a healthy EQ?

15

FAITH UNDERSTANDS HOW TO ASK BETTER QUESTIONS

BIBLICAL PERSPECTIVES

> *But the Lord God called out to the man and said to him, "Where are you?"* (Genesis 3:9).
>
> *Then the Lord said to Cain, "Where is your brother Abel?"* (Genesis 4:9).
>
> *Then the Lord answered Job out of the whirlwind: "Who is this that darkens counsel by words without knowledge? Gird up your loins, like a man. I will question you, and you shall declare to me. Where were you when I laid the foundation of the earth? Tell me, if you have understanding"* (Job 38:1-4).
>
> *"Is it lawful to pay taxes to the emperor, or not? Should we pay them, or should we not?" But knowing their hypocrisy, he said to them, "Why are you putting me to the test? Bring me a denarius and let me see it." And they brought one. Then he said to them, "Whose head is this, and whose title?"* (Mark 12:14-16).

I have heard many declare that the Bible is God's great answer book. In one sense, this is true, unless you mean by that a series of declarations and proclamations. The Bible is really a great confession of faith by those, in the Hebrew Scriptures, who found themselves encountered by God and, in the Christian Scriptures, those who experienced God in the person of his son, Jesus of Nazareth. Repeating: it is not the story of those who found God but the story of those who concluded God had found them. Coming to grips with what this encounter means for the life of the nation Israel and for the lives of those under Roman occupation proves to be exciting, inspiring, unpredictable, and explosive. They don't meet a God who can be tamed or easily fitted into the parameters of current religious understandings.

They meet a God who has a lot of questions. In fact, it is not exaggerating to refer to the Bible as God's great question book. I once did back-to-back sermon series on "Old Testament Questions" and "Questions Jesus Asked." If you have not explored these questions, you will be surprised at their diversity and disturbing explorations. To this day, Jewish teaching relies heavily on asking good questions and helping students learn to ask better questions. A book of answers is, in some sense, a closed book. No discussion is necessary. No wider frames of reference need be called it. Everything is settled and over. No more thinking or exploring are necessary. This is certainly not the nature of Holy Scripture, which is why it continues to be argued, discussed, debated, and analyzed. On every page there is the call for reflection and conversation. It is almost God's invitation, "Let's sit down together and talk things over." This seems close to what God asks in Isaiah 1:18 – *Come now and let us reason together, saith the Lord* (KJV) or as the NRSV translates: *Come now, let us argue it out, says the Lord.*

Early in the biblical story, two great questions form the basis for all that is to follow. Both are God's questions: *Where are you in relation to me?* (Genesis 3:9). *Where are you in relation to other people?* (Genesis 4:9). Jesus speaks to both of these questions when he responds to the question about the greatest commandment: "*You shall love the Lord you God with all your heart, and will all your soul, and with all your mind, and with all your strength and you shall love your neighbor as yourself*" (Mark 12:30-31). The Bible is all about our relationship with God and our relationship with one another. That is why I tell people I have a Relational Theology.

Faith Never Stands Alone

In Mark 12, Jesus shows himself the expert in asking better questions when, asked about paying taxes, asks whose image is on the coin used for paying such taxes. In response to a loaded question (as most political questions are), he redirects the question to the reality of the world in which the nation lived. In Job 38, God's response to the request from Job to have his questions answered, is to plummet him with ultimate questions that reveal Job's lack of an adequate frame of reference in which to place his questions.

Faith always has lots of questions; that's the easy part. For faith to be on the grow, we have to learn how to ask better questions.

Exploring and Considering

> From the rich heritage of Jewish interpretation, I learned the mysteries and contradictions of Scripture weren't meant to be fought against but courageously engaged, and that the Bible by its very nature invites us to wrestle, doubt, imagine, and debate.[161]

The classic wrestling match in Scripture is the one in which Jacob engages (Genesis 32:24-32). When the match is over, Jacob confesses, *"I have seen God, face to face."* There is much to wrestle over as Jacob makes his way back to, hopefully, make peace with the brother he cheated out of the family blessing. Stolen blessings can't cut it, so a large part of this wrestling match is to secure a blessing that is truly his own. A new name comes with that blessing along with one of the most surprising announcements in Scripture: *"Your name will no longer be Jacob. It will be Israel because you have struggled with God and with men and have prevailed"* (Genesis 32:28). I wonder how often, when we have felt the need for prayer, if we had been listening closely, God would have said, "Let's wrestle."

That is certainly one of the best ways to better questions.

> In fact, learning we pretty quickly come to see, is seldom about correct answers…the kids start to see "why" matters far more than "what."

---

[161] Rachel Held Evans, *Inspired*, xix.

And I'll prod them. I'll encourage questions, which matter more than answers. I'll praise an eagerness to explore and original thinking, and risky thinking, but not jump-off-the-cliff thinking.[162]

This is the kind of teacher who has interesting classes! If all that matters is answers, memorization will do the trick. The problem is that life is not a matter of true/false, multiple choice, or fill-in-the-blank answers. It is far too complex for such simplicity. It calls for exploration, original thinking and, especially, risky thinking. "Why?" is usually what sends us off in these directions; "what?" is a dead-end street; no further thinking is required.

> Rather than seeking to provide definitive answers, our faith communities should be creating the safe spaces where we can ask the difficult questions, admit our struggles, and hold one another up in loving support and accountability when we fall short.[163]
>
> My parents responded to my questions with compassion, but the evangelical community around me treated me like a wildfire in need of containment.[164]

If you are permitted to ask only the "safe" questions, not much dialogue or learning is going to occur. If "Don't rock the boat" is the motto for a Sunday School class, that boat will forever remain docked and won't take the students into any new waters. Taking the risk to ask the disturbing questions can only be done when you know a safe place has been provided for such questions and those gathered are committed to learning and growing together. If I only expect to hear what I already know and believe, remaining home would probably be the best option. Jesus' method of teaching with parables presented his audience with issues that required further thinking and discussion. That is why some of his parables got him into so much trouble. They were not calming devotional

---

162 David McCullough, *You Are Not Special* (New York: ECCO, 2014), 74, 80.
163 Christian Platt, *Post Christian*, 87.
164 Rachel Held Evans, *Inspired*, xvii.

thoughts; they were challenges and opportunities to send life in another direction.

> We have found inspiration in writings by Peter Drucker, who grasped more than fifty years ago the power of changing what you ask. "The important and difficult job is never to find the right answers," he wrote. "It is to find the right question. For there are few things as useless – if not dangerous – as the right answer to the wrong question."[165]

Sometimes people ask the wrong question because it is the only one to which they have a good answer. Often in a meeting I have wanted to say, "Yes, that is good advice, if that is the right question." The one who asks the questions shapes the discussion. Only right questions can lead to the relevant discussion. In reading a novel about the great London plague of 1665, the questions asked were all about how to prevent its spread; the major questions were not about its origin. Here is how the wrong question can lead to outrageous answers:

> "Remove your hat." "My hat?" asked Chaloner warily. "Fancy Cavalier head pieces are attractive to plague-bearing vapors," the physician replied with considerable conviction. "Whereas plain, modest ones are not."[166]
>
> "We only sing," he informed Chaloner. "Because instruments are more likely to summon up the pestilence than unaccompanied voices." Chaloner blinked his astonishment to this claim. "Are they?" Paget nodded earnestly. "They set up vibrations that attract deadly miasmas. It is a scientific fact. However, there are no vibrations with singing, so we are safe."[167]
>
> The plague measures, which did indeed include setting huge bonfires to purify the air, had only limited success, because neither the authorities nor the medical profession understood

---

165 Hal Gregersen, *Questions Are the Answer,* 3.
166 Susanna Gregory, *The Executioner of St. Paul's* (London: Sphere, 2017), 155.
167 Ibid, 62-63.

what they were dealing with. The fire raged for three days in early September, until a chanced downpour put them out.[168]

The "remedies" and preventatives listed in *The Approved Plague Physitian* include London Treacle, *sal mirabilis,* smoking and chewing tobacco, and if all else failed, the author recommended "a Godly and Penitent Prayer Unto Almighty God, for our preservation, and Deliverance Therefrom."[169]

The greatest irony is that, because dogs and cats were suspected carriers, they were eliminated from London. The black rats with their fleas, the source of the plague, were allowed to flourish. It seems there was not enough basic medical and scientific knowledge to know how to frame questions about the origin of the plague. As a result, as many as 100,000 lives may have been lost in London alone. The wrong question was dangerous beyond imagination.

Quotes Worth Thinking About

> Pictured in a cartoon is a couple at a table. The man says, "Let me interrupt your expertise with my confidence." In theory, confidence and competence go hand in hand. In practice they often diverge.[170]

Competent answers are meant to follow competent questions. Unfortunately, there appears much confidence in the media with a woeful lack of expertise. Along with "who's giving that answer?", I also like to ask, "who's asking that question?" When the Scribes and Pharisees asked Jesus a question, more often than not, it was meant to lay a trap. Jesus was always perceptive enough to recognize a dangerous question and his reply was usually a different question. Today, asking better questions requires a skill that comes with knowledge, respect, and honest motives.

---

168 Ibid, 453.
169 Ibid, 454.
170 Adam Grant, *Think Again,* 37.

My journeying with the characters in the famous *Peanuts* comic strip continues. *The Peanuts Papers* is a collection by "Writers and Cartoonists on Charlie Brown, Snoopy & the Gang, and the Meaning of Life." Nicole Rudick, in a chapter titled "A Space for Thinking," makes this observation:[171]

> The main truth Schultze tells is that there are not answers to the really big questions. The strips achievement and a significant reason for its longevity, is in its creation of a space of inquiry that is never closed off.

That's what better questions always do: they create a space of inquiry that is never closed off. These are the questions that invite conversation and dialogue. Dogmatic questions are only seeking confirmation, not interaction or further questions. Either you accept the answers that are implied in the question or that you know they are looking for, or you don't. Open-ended questions encourage a thinking-together that keeps the space of inquiry open. "Questions, when they are seen as sincere requests for help, invite creative contributions from others rather than merely campaigning for their support. They engage and energize."[172]

Thomas C. Foster in *How to Read Literature Like a Professor,* maintains that books have lives of their own. "More often than not, the punctuation following the final sentence is a period. It should be a question mark, though, because what occurs from then on is anybody's guess."[173] Many novels I have read have that period, but you know it is not meant to be the end of the story. The reader is left to ponder what really might be coming next. The question mark invites the reader to be a participant in the writing of the story yet to come. The period, perhaps, is too much like the ending of most Warner Brothers cartoons, "That's all folks!" Something within us always likes to know that's not all there is.

---

171 Andrew Blauner, ed., *The Peanuts Papers*, 42.
172 Hal Gregersen, *Questions Are the Answer,* 28.
173 Thomas C. Foster, *How to Read Literature Like a Professor* (New York: Harper Business, 2018), 28.

Going north on IH-35, I saw it – the billboard announces that Mother Someone (let's just call her "Mama") has the answers to all your questions. I suppose Mama patiently sits and fully answers all questions or reads palms, probably, for a fee. In matters of faith, however, are we spiritually richer with answers to hard questions or with greater inquiry?[174]

The enrichment of our spiritual lives is much more dependent on greater inquiry than answers to hard questions. The Sermon on the Mount provides the outline for the way Kingdom citizens live, not by giving answers to the hard questions, but by inviting reflection, conversation, meditation, and further questions. You never find Jesus giving "Seven Keys to a Happy Life." He tells stories that raise many more questions than simple answers. The great mystics of the past never came to final conclusions about everything in life; they continued to be seekers and questioners. The full and meaningful life is not found by the one who has all the answers, it is discovered by the one who knows which questions will bring the kind of pondering that enriches and refines.

COMING TO SOME CONCLUSIONS

> Einstein: "If I had an hour to solve a problem and my life depended on the solution, I would spend the first fifty-five minutes determining the proper question to ask, for once I know the proper question, I could solve the problem in less than five minutes."[175]

I immediately thought of what I had read about Gertrude Stein, who on her deathbed, is said to have asked, "What is the answer?" Then after a long silence, she asked, "What is the question?" Frederick Buechner provides this information and this comment:
We tend to lose track of the questions about things that matter always, life-and-death questions as about meaning purpose and

---

174 Walt Shelton, *The Daily Practice of Life*, 21.
175 Hal Gregersen, *Questions Are the Answer*, 22.

Faith Never Stands Alone

value. To lose track of such deep questions as these is to risk losing track of who we really are in our own depths and where we are really going.[176]

The better questions of faith are always about things that really matter, things that really are life-and-death questions. That is why I found so much satisfaction in pastoral ministry. I was able to deal with things that really mattered as people faced the issues of life that brought up the big questions. There are many such lists to be found, but this list of the fundamental questions of existence seems as good as they get:[177]

1. *Who are we?* – the question of identity.
2. *Where did we come from?* – the question of origin.
3. *Where are we going?* – the question of destiny.
4. *Why are we here?* – the question of purpose.
5. *What ultimately matters?* – the question of meaning.
6. *How are we to live?* – the question of morality/right action.
7. *What happens when we die?* – the question of finality and continuity.

These are questions worth our reflection and conversation and can be guides as we attempt to frame better questions to deal with the many issues we face.

QUESTIONS FOR REFLECTION AND CONVERSATION

1. Have you considered the advantages of better questions?
2. Do you agree that the one who asks the questions shapes the discussion?
3. Have you ever been in a situation where confidence overruled expertise?

---

176 Frederick Buechner, *Listening to Your Life*, 124.
177 Michael Dowd, *Thank God for Evolution*, 15.

16

Faith Has Nothing to Do With Perfection

Biblical Perspectives

> *' 'Simon, Simon, listen! Satan has demanded to sift all of you like wheat, but I have prayed for you that your own faith may not fail; and you, when once you have turned back, strengthen your brothers." And he said to him, "Lord, I am ready to go with you to prison and to death!" Jesus said, "I tell you, Peter, the cock will not crow this day, until you have denied three times that you know me"* (Luke 22:31-34).
>
> *"You will all fall away," Jesus told them…Peter declared, "Even if all fall away, I will not"* (Mark 14:27, 29, TNIV).
>
> *Since all have sinned and fall short of the glory of God* (Romans 3:23).

Even a cursive reading of the Gospels reveals that Jesus did not select perfect men to be his disciples. There were some in the religious culture who thought they were, like Mary Poppins, "practically perfect in every way." They were absolutely not disciple material; they would never have understood how much they had to learn. Jesus chose human beings, sinners who frequently missed the mark and fell short of the glory God intended in their lives (a good definition of the Greek word translated "sin"). At no point does Scripture indicate we will ever have a 100% bullseye record or that the glory of God's image in each of will ever totally shine.

When Jesus announced that all of his disciples would fall away when he is arrested, tried, and crucified, they, no doubt, were shocked by the low expectations Jesus had for them. Of course, they had no idea of the terror that was about to unfold. Naturally, Peter spoke up and said something like, "I've had my doubts about some of these other fellows, but you can absolutely count on me to loyal and stick with you all the way through." I don't doubt his sincerity; I doubt his apprehension of how such events would strike deep emotional chords of fear.

All the Gospels report that someone drew a sword and cut off the ear of the high priest's servant. Only John's Gospel tells us that Peter, who had a sword, was that person. His courage at the beginning is evident but this is a small matter in relationship to what is coming.

Only Luke gives the warning and a promise delivered to Peter. I believe the translation by Kenneth Wuest captures the full meaning of what was said. In the preface to his translation, Wuest writes:

> This translation of the New Testament, unlike the standard translations such as the Authorized Version of 1611 and the American Revised Version of 1901, uses as many English words as are necessary to bring out the richness, force, and clarity of the Greek text. The result is what I have called an expanded translation. It is intended as a companion to, or commentary on, the standard translations (WUEST, vii).

Here is Wuest's expanded translation of Luke 22:31-32:

> *Simon, Simon, behold, Satan by asking obtained you and your fellow disciples for himself and from my power to his, in order that he may shake you in a sieve as grain is sifted, by an inward agitation, trying your faith to the verge of overthrow. But as for myself, I made petition concerning you that your faith should not be totally eclipsed. And as for you, when you have returned to your original position with respect to your faith, stabilize your brethren* (WUEST).

I have not found a commentary that captures any better what I believe to be the meaning of what Jesus says. Some have doubted that Jesus' prayer for Peter is answered. I am convinced the prayer is answered because Peter's faith is not "overthrown." The next time the disciples gathered, I believe they meet a humbler Simon Peter who is quite certain he is just like all them in his humanity and, as such, is in a much better position to be a stabilizing force.

Nowhere does Scripture cite any perfect people of faith and nowhere does it call for such perfection. The frequently misunderstood reference in Matthew 5:48, *Be perfect, therefore, as your heavenly Father is perfect,* has nothing to do with moral or ethical perfection. *Perfect* means wholeness or completeness. Two better and more accurate translations are: *You, then, must become complete – as your heavenly Father is complete* (NEW) and *Therefore, as for you, you shall be those who are complete in your character, even as your Father in heaven is complete in His being* (WUEST).

EXPLORING AND CONSIDERING

> I don't know whether it is time or history or Calvin that has left me so profoundly convinced of the importance of human fallibility, and so struck by its peculiar character. But I wouldn't mind hearing the word "sin" once in a while.[178]

I hardly ever hear anyone in the news confess "sin." I hear a lot about mistakes, poor judgment, and bad choices. All of these reflect the human fallibility that has the biblical tag of sin. When David is confronted by the prophet Nathan for his double deeds of murder and adultery, his response is: *"I have sinned against the Lord"* (2 Samuel 12:13). Even after these seemingly unforgivable acts, David can still be called a man after God's own heart (1 Samuel 13:14): he acknowledged exactly what he done was wrong, he called it out for what it was, he repented, and attempted to get back on track with his life. The tragedy is, his life was never again the

---

178 Marilynne Robinson, *The Givenness of Things*, 101.

same, not because of retribution on God's part, but as the result of the playing out of the consequences of his deeds.

> No decent AA meeting ever began with, "Hi, my name is Rachel, and I totally have my act together."[179].

We keep missing the mark; we keep failing to permit our being created in the image of God shape our character and conduct; we keep demonstrating our human fallibility despite our best efforts at cover ups. AA is regularly a place of healing and transformation because it is a place of honest confession of the grip that alcohol has on the lives of those present. Confession of what is often termed our "human predicament" is the confession that we need God and we need one another. To be human is not a sin. To be human is the confession that we are sinners but are seeking to live daily with God's forgiveness, mercy, and grace.

> Dickens is the most human writer you'll ever read. He believes in people, even with all their faults, and he slings a great story, with the most memorable characters you'll meet anywhere.[180]

That's the way I feel when I read the Bible. God believes in people even with all their faults and the Bible slings a great story with the most memorable characters you'll meet anywhere. God's forgiveness, grace, mercy, and love are writ large on every page, and the people whose stories are told experience their great days and their fallibility days. But God never gives up on them – or us. I was ever so grateful the day I found a more literal translation of the last verse of Psalm 23. Instead of, *Surely goodness and mercy shall follow me all the days of my life,"* I read, *Surely goodness and mercy shall pursue me all the days of my life"* (HOLMAN). I have used that text in a sermon with the line: "God is after you. God is after you with his goodness and mercy. Let him overtake you. You'll never regret it."

---

179 Rachel Held Evans, *Searching*, 70.
180 Thomas C. Foster, *How to Read Literature Like a Professor*, 310.

Barry Schwartz thinks that what prevents a lot of young people from developing a serious career interest is unrealistic expectations. They're holding out for perfection.[181]

The day I decided I would never find the perfect church was very close to the day I confessed I would never be the perfect pastor. Unrealistic expectations are part and parcel of so many things in life; in extreme cases this leads to cynicism and despair. We need to set goals and have dreams but expecting the impossible is not a healthy perspective. The Bible is full of flawed characters who did amazing things, not perfect things, but amazing things considering their flaws. Although I have not read the book, the title has long fascinated me: *The Joy of Imperfection* by Damon Zahariades. The subtitle is: *A Stress Free Guide to Silencing Your Inner Critic, Conquering Perfection, and Becoming the Best Version of Yourself.* A book I do own and have read is *The Spirituality of Imperfection* by Ernest Kurtz and Katherine Ketcham. It could be termed a self-help book but it certainly has a spiritual emphasis as the title implies. Here is one of my favorite stories from a chapter titled: "The Reality of Limitation":

> A priest of the Greek Orthodox Church, Father Thomas Hopko, tells of a monk he met on Mount Athos. He was in a very bad state, very dark, very bitter, very angry. When asked what was the matter, he said, "Look at me; I've been here for thirty-eight years, and I have not yet attained pure prayer." And this other fellow on the pilgrimage was saying how sad he thought it was. Another man present said, "It's a sad story all right, but the sadness consists in the fact that after thirty-eight years in a monastery he's still interested in pure prayer."[182]

---

181 Angelia Duckworth, *Grit,* 107.
182 Ernest Kurtz and Katherine Ketcham, *The Spirituality of Imperfection* (New York: Harper Perennial, 2014), 310.

Quotes Worth Thinking About

> He'd mentored a high-achieving Finnish girl recently, "an A plus-plus-plus-plus student," who'd had a nightmare trying to launch a start-up. School had made her a perfectionist, but the world demanded flexibility. The "education system was all about right answers," he added. "Life is not about right answers."[183]

Faith is not about A plus-plus-plus-plus spirituality that has all the right answers. This seems to have been what the Pharisees and Scribes believed was required in the religious life of their day. Jesus' practice of flexibility was quite upsetting to the rigidity of a system built on the perfect keeping of the Law. The faith that Jesus demonstrated and encouraged was not based on perfection but human need and imperfection. He didn't always give the "right" answers; he always gave the best answers that came from grace and love. In an imperfect and broken world, he knew what was needed.

> "What kind of a name is that, anyway? Dismas?"
>
> Dismas Hardy responded: "Dismas was the good thief, crucified up on Calvary, next to Jesus. He's the patron saint of thieves and murderers, which is handy if you happen to be a defense attorney. It's always good to have a saint on your home team."[184]

The statement is meant to be tongue-in-cheek by the hero of this mystery novel. While not to be taken literally, it is always good to know somebody who understands when you fall, when you fail, when you sin. When Paul writes in 2 Corinthians 5:18 – *All this is from God, who reconciled us to himself through Christ, and has given us the ministry of reconciliation,* he placed the emphasis on mercy and grace, not on judgment. The story we call the Parable of the Prodigal Son (Luke 15:11-32) disturbs some people because it is so short on judgment and so long on reconciliation. The prodigal has become the patron saint for those who get lost and don't know how

---

183 Alex Beard, *Natural Born Learners,* 129-130.
184 John Lescroart, *The Rule of Law* (New York: Atria Paperback, 2019), 105.

to get back home; he shows us the way. The elder brother is more like a prosecuting attorney – no help there, only a swift kick out of the father's house. To the chagrin of the righteous, Jesus threw open the doors of the Father's house; those doors remain open today.

Coming to Some Conclusions

Perhaps a good summary of what we have discussed comes from the teaching of Agnes Sanford:

> We were to believe in spite of not believing. That was what faith was all about, she told us. "Lord, I believe; help thou mine unbelief," said the father of the sick son (Mark 9:24), and though it wasn't much, Jesus considered it enough.[185]

Whatever we can do, the most we can muster, the best achievements we can make – all imperfectly done – surely will be considered enough. Our faith is not on trial, only our sincerely seeking to respond to God's grace and love to the best of our ability. I would probably add: all things considered. Who knows what heartache and disappointing efforts had gone into the father's attempts to find a remedy for his son's epilepsy (which had been with him since childhood)? How many faith healers had he already tried? Maybe that's why the father said, *"If you are able to do anything, have pity on us and help us"* (Mark 9:22). I'd like to make a plaque based on Agnes Sanford's words: "Though it wasn't much, Jesus considered it enough." Why not? Faith has nothing to do with perfection anyway.

Questions for Reflection and Conversation

1. What do you think are the lessons to be learned from Peter's experience?
2. Why do you think speakers at AA meetings begin the way they do?
3. What things in this chapter spoke to you in a personal way?

---

185 Frederick Buechner, *Listening to Your Life*, 1.

17

Justice and Compassion Are Necessary for "Good Faith"

Biblical Perspectives

You pay tithes on mint, fennel, and caraway seed, and leave neglected the weightier matters of the Law – justice, compassion, and good faith (Matthew 23:23, TAUSSIG).

He has told you, O mortal, what is good; and what does the Lord require of you but to do justice, and to love kindness, and to walk humbly with your God (Micah 6:8).

Cease to do evil, learn to do good; seek justice, rescue the oppressed, defend the orphan, plead for the widow (Isaiah 1:16b-17).

Ah, you who make iniquitous decrees, who write oppressive statutes, to turn aside the needy from justice and to rob the poor of my people of their right… (Isaiah 10:1-2).

This was the guilt of your sister Sodom: she and her daughters had pride, excess of food, and prosperous ease, but did not aid the poor and needy. They were haughty, and did abominable things before me, therefore I removed them when I saw it (Ezekiel 16:49-50).

Come, you that are blessed by my Father, inherit the kingdom prepared for you from the foundation of the world; for I was hungry and you gave me food, I was thirsty and you gave me something to drink, I was a stranger and you welcomed me, I was naked and you gave me clothing, I was sick and you took care of me, I was in prison and you visited me (Matthew 25:34-36).

It is true that the Bible never uses the term "social justice," but its pages are filled with prophetic condemnations of those who neglect the poor and needy in their communities. Jesus lists the weightier matters of the law as justice, compassion, and good faith. I don't think it is a misreading of the text to assert that justice and compassion are ingredients in good faith. In the disturbing parable found in Matthew 25, Jesus selects the hungry, the thirsty, the stranger, the naked, the sick, and the prisoners as the least in society where he waits to be discovered in them. *"I tell you that all those things you have done for one who was least in my family, you have also done for me"* (Matthew 25:41, BARNSTONE).

What I find most enlightening (or disturbing) is the reference from Ezekiel. The prophet precedes his words with the traditional note, *"Hear the word of the Lord"* (Ezekiel 16:35). Almost every sermon I ever heard on Sodom gave only one reason for the cause of its destruction. When God has his prophet give the guilt-list of Sodom, he begins with their greed, food surplus, and wealth which they did not use to help the poor and needy. What we call social justice topped the sin-list for Sodom. Then God adds that they are haughty. Last on his list is that they *did abominable things* (Ezekiel 16:50).

Exploring and Considering

> The reservations to which Indians were removed were in regions which offered few apparent energy resources. They were moved to the dry Great Plains. There the vanishing buffalo was an anticipation of what many whites hoped would be the vanishing Indian.[186]
>
> Across the South, someone was hanged or burned alive every four days from 1889 to 1929, according to the 1933 book *The Tragedy of Lynching,* for such alleged crimes as "steal-

---

186 Martin E. Marty, *When Faiths Collide,* 55.

ing hogs, horse-stealing, poisoning mules, jumping labor contracts, suspected of killing cattle, boastful remarks" or "trying to act like a white person." Sixty-six were killed after being accused of "insult to a white person." One was killed for stealing seventy-five-cents.[187]

When we think about justice, we cannot ignore the injustice that was dispensed to Native Americans and African Americans. The record is a tragic one, both for the perpetrators and for those bystanders who raised little protest. *Bury My Heart at Wounded Knee* by Dee Brown reveals the "systematic plunder of the American Indians during the second half of the nineteenth century, battle by battle, massacre, broken treaty by broken treaty."[188] It parallels Isabel Wilkerson's *The Warmth of Other Suns* from which the second of the above quotes is taken. Both of these books are painful to read because the wrongs are wrong beyond our imagination. Both deserve the label we put on the Holocaust: "Never Again!"

The biblical prophets found it a never-ending battle for fair and compassionate treatment of the powerless. For almost all of human history, the cliché about the Golden Rule has proved true: "Those who have the gold, make the rules." And the rules are always in favor of the powerful. Following the Civil War and the emancipation of slaves, some plantation owners found ways to keep slave labor. Many former slaves became sharecroppers, but experienced what John Starling did at harvest-time. Isabel Wilkerson relates that frequently the planter reported a good year because they broke even. Therefore, the planter insisted that he owed John nothing. Many worked all year for nothing.[189]

> Most other sharecroppers ended deeper in debt than before. "They could never leave as long as they owed the master," John Starling's son said. "That made the planter as much

---

187 Isabel Wilkerson, *The Warmth of Oher Suns* (New York: Vantage Books, 2011), 39.
188 Dee Brown, *Bury My Heart at Wounded Knee* (New York: Holt, Rinehart & Winston, 1970), inside front cover.
189 Isabel Wilkerson, *The Warmth of Other Suns*, 52.

master as any master during slavery, because the sharecropper was bound to him, belonged to him, almost like a slave."[190]

There were many voices raised in condemnation of such a system but none persuasive enough to go against the culture or move elected officials to action. There are always those who cry, "The sharecroppers could have done something about it if they had really wanted to." Some could and did. Many could not. Blanket condemnation of the poor and powerless is the easy way to justify a do-nothing policy. All too often, there is prejudice (pre-judgment) against those in need. Of course, there are always those who abuse a system of welfare, as there are those of extreme wealth who find ways to avoid paying any (or few) taxes. Such is the nature of humanity. But that does not mean there are not people who are in real need and are powerless and helpless to do anything about it. It is difficult for most of us to understand what it's like not to have a voice that will be heard.

> Between 1604 and 1905 almost eleven thousand square miles of land were "enclosed" by Acts of Parliament in the United Kingdom. Land once farmed and enjoyed by the community was fenced off to produce higher yields, and rents were increased. As a result, many peasants were forced away from their homes to seek work in towns and cities, causing huge disruption, dispossession, and discontent, which, in turn culminated in major riots in the 1830s.[191]

The above are the author's notes from her novel. I believe the impact of this book in story form is much greater than if it had been simply a record of what had occurred. You come to know people whose lives are changed, and often shattered, by a system that they are powerless to do anything about. A meeting is called for the purpose of discussing the enclosing acts that were rapidly taking away

---

190 Ibid, 54.
191 Tessa Harris, *Shadow of the Raven* (New York: Kensington Books, 2015), ix-x.

the remaining community land. When the meeting was about to end, something occurs that, I fear, happens far too often.

> Thomas heard a rumpus from somewhere in the far corner. He craned his neck. A laboring man, Will Ketch, was elbowing his way to the front. "I would speak!" cried the workman hoarsely. "I would speak for the commoners!" Nicholas Lupton shot Sir Montagu a look, then nodded to a bald-headed man who had been standing at his side throughout the proceedings. "Commoners have no right to speak!" the steward called loudly over the din. As Ketch approached, the bald guard grabbed him by his arm and forced it behind his back. Another burly man assisted him and together they dispatched the cowman, cussing and shouting, from the room.[192]

It is not unusual for the exploited to have no right to speak. Keeping them silenced is a major tactic for keeping the powerful in control. The advantage of learning about this dark period in British history in a novel, is that you find yourself responding emotionally to these commoners. You wonder why those in charge of the meeting had no mercy or compassion for a fellow human being. There you have it: they did not recognize them as fellow human beings. They were inferiors. They were the less deserving. They were those of low birth and low worth. As long as you can keep thinking of them in this way, you know they have no right to speak, they have nothing worth hearing.

> It is no longer about being correct. It is about being connected. Being in right relationship is much, much better than just trying to be "right."[193]

When the expert in Torah Law asked, "*Who is my neighbor?*", Jesus responded with a parable that changed the question. The question became: "To whom should I be a neighbor?" The simple answer: to anyone who needs a neighbor, to anyone you meet on the road of life who is wounded, to anyone others are passing by.

---

192 Ibid, 135.
193 Richard Rohr, *The Universal Christ,* 168.

I know this raises all kinds of logistical questions, but the answer is that my neighbor includes all in my neighborhood. We are all co-neighbors.

David McCullough tells about his awkward beginning teaching in Hawaii. The turn-around came when he read the class Stephen Crane's short story *The Open Boat*. The story captured the imagination of the class and literally brought it to life. McCullough writes this about the story:

> "The Open Boat" is a vivid allegory of the human condition. The dinghy is the planet. The threatening but indifferent ocean is the universe. The unnamed men are you and me. Their only chance comes through vigilance, perseverance, concern for one another and unity. It's all about the harsh realities of life where shipwrecks happen, train wrecks, car crashes, earthquakes, etc. We are inclined to ask, "Why?" A better question is, "Why anybody?" We are all in the same boat.[194]

You can understand why the story brought about so much discussion. It should continue to bring about that same kind of discussion in a culture where many appear to have forgotten the bottom line of existence: we are all in this thing together.

Quotes Worth Thinking About

> My father said when he walked into his father's church after they came back from the army, the first thing he saw was a piece of needlework hanging on the wall above the communion table. It was very beautifully done, flowers, and flames surrounding the words "The Lord Our God is a Purifying Fire." He stood there looking at it, visibly displeased by it, apparently, because one of the women said to him, "It's just a bit of Scripture." He said, "I beg your pardon, ma'am. No, that is not Scripture." "Well," she said, "then it certainly ought to be."[195]

---

194 David McCullough, *You Are Not Special*, 274-277.
195 Marilynne Robinson, *Gilead*, 113.

It is almost impossible to imagine how anyone who has come to know the God who has revealed himself most clearly in the person of Jesus, could believe that a purifying fire is what best represents him at the communion table. What kind of life, faith, and church experiences could cause one to want this to be Scripture? Much fear, anger, and judgment can be read into such a desire. The community of faith she represents seems to have been short on mercy, compassion, and grace and, thereby, very short on biblical justice.

> Yet my own snobbery couldn't protect me from being drawn, more deeply, into the place. I had to admit that these people, with all their specific flaws intact, had opened the door to grace…because they believed in the absolute religious value of welcoming people who didn't belong.[196]

When we finally decide that everybody belongs, that everybody should have a place at the same table, we are ready for the kind of justice called for in Scripture.

Coming to Some Conclusions

Perhaps this chapter on justice represents one of the most difficult aspects of the life of faith. There are times when we need to make our voices heard and speak up for those whose voices are ignored. When we do, we enter high risk territory. When oppression and dehumanization are in operation, we need to be among those who echo the biblical teaching that every single person on earth is created in the image of God and needs to be treated with the worth that is deserved.

We cannot solve all the problems and inequities in the world, nor are we called to do so. We cannot help everybody, everywhere. We cannot give to every worthy cause that seeks donations for its work (each month I now receive 150 requests for contributions). I can help some people in need. I can give to some causes. There is always some aspect of the call for justice to which I can respond.

---

196 Sara Miles, *Take This Bread*, 81.

That response will vary according to my ability and the opportunity that is open for my participation. I am grateful to have a church community that makes a large place for ministry beyond its walls. It provides channels for participation that go far beyond what I can do as an individual. I am privileged to be a part of that community because it helps me stay connected to the larger community that literally encompasses the world.

Addendum

The purpose of this book is to provide material on certain aspects of the life of faith for reflection and discussion. The subject of justice must include Christian nonviolence. It is a subject too large for much exploration in these few pages. However, I would like to suggest a resource for those who are interested in a succinct and excellent summary. It is an essay by Thomas Merton in *Passion for Peace*. William Shannon has brought together Merton's principle social essays on non-violence, war, and racism. The essay is the result of a request to write an article on "Demut" (Humility), "which turned out to be really an essay on the beatitude of the Meek, as applied to Christian nonviolence." [197] Merton writes:

> Nonviolence must be realistic and concrete. Like ordinary political action, it is no more than the "art of the possible." But precisely the advantage of nonviolence is that is has a *more Christian and more humane notion of what is possible*. Where the powerful believe that only power is efficacious, the nonviolent resister is persuaded of the superior efficacy of love, openness, peaceful negotiation and above all of truth.[198]

---

[197] Thomas Merton, William H. Shannon, ed., *Passion for Peace* (New York: Crossroad, 1996), 249.
[198] Ibid, 254.

QUESTIONS FOR REFLECTION AND CONVERSATION

1. What was most difficult for you as you read this chapter?
2. How do you interpret Jesus' parable in Matthew 25?'
3. Do you think Merton's ideas on Christian non-violence are applicable to our time?

18

FAITH IS A "WHATEVER" STANCE

BIBLICAL PERSPECTIVES

Come now, you who "Today or tomorrow we will go to such and such a town and spend a year there, doing business and making money." Yet you do not even know what tomorrow will bring (James 4:13).

Do not boast about tomorrow, for you do not know what a day may bring (Proverbs 27:1).

I know what it is to have little, and I know what it is to have plenty. In any and all circumstances I have learned the secret of being well-fed and of going hungry, of having plenty and of being in need. I can do all things through him who strengthens me (Philippians 4:12-13).

To the present hour we are hungry and thirsty, we are poorly clothed and beaten and homeless, and we grow weary from the work of our own hands. When reviled, we bless; when persecuted, we endure; when slandered, we speak kindly. We have become like the rubbish of the world, the dregs of all things, to this very day (1 Corinthians 4:11-13).

I almost titled this chapter "There is a lot of acceptance and surrender in faith." The future is always filled with uncertainties and both the Hebrew and Christian Scriptures remind us of one of life's basics: we never know what will happen tomorrow (Proverbs 27:1 and James 4:13). Now in the middle of my eighth decade, I confess to the many tomorrows that were so unlike anything I had expected or planned for. When Paul talks about the fluctuating circumstances he experienced, he shares his "secret" of meeting the challenge of life's ups and downs. It seems his secret was the determination to live fully with whatever and wherever he found himself and not be thrown off course by bemoaning what should be. Life offered him sudden reversals in his missionary journeys and he accepted and surrendered to each one by maintaining his confidence in God's provisions and doing whatever was necessary to keep going.

Exploring and Considering

> Very soon I would learn that one great task still lay ahead of me, one thing that – more than any other would define my life. Late one afternoon, a few weeks hence, I would be dragged back into the secret world and any hope I had of reaching for normal would be gone, probably forever. Like people say – if you want to make God laugh, tell him you've got plans.[199]

Once again, a novel takes a well-known saying and places it in the context of a situation with which we can all identify. For the story's hero, the future was going to be different because a new challenge meant a new responsibility that was going to send life in a new direction. Life and faith became a "whatever" because it meant whatever was necessary. It is impossible for us to know or plan for all of the "whatevers" we will encounter as we move forward. A willingness to be flexible and the ability to adapt helps us to be ready for the "whatevers".

> Now I really rejoice when something does not go as I wish – because I see that He wants our trust – that is why in the loss let us praise God as if we have got everything.[200]

---

199 Terry Hayes, *I Am Pilgrim*, 66.
200 Mother Teresa, *Come Be My Light*, 24.

Faith Never Stands Alone

"I did it my way," sounds like a person who has taken charge of his life (in this case, Frank Sinatra), but the real questions are: Do I know what is best for me? Do I know the right way that will lead to the things I really need? Mother Teresa had plans, she had preferred ways for things to work out, but when those did not materialize, she trusted that God had something better in mind. She lived her life not by expectations but by trusting in God's providence. Making the best of what we do not perceive as the best is the key to living creatively and redemptively with less than we had hoped for. It may, in the long run, turn out to be more than we had hoped for.

My friend Perry Bramlett brought me much wisdom from the pen of C. S. Lewis (and it was literally from his pen because he never used a typewriter). In a letter to a friend, C. S. Lewis wrote that "the real business of a Christian was not to succeed, but to *do right* and leave the rest to God."[201] What we leave to God is the whatever. We do what we believe we need to do, to the best our limited ability, and then leave the rest to God. It's not a matter of whether we succeed or fail, feel good or bad about it, or fail to see any immediate results of any kind. Trusting *that in all things God works for the good of those who love him, who have been called according to his purpose* (Romans 8:28, TNIV), frees us from having to keep tabs on results. My favorite translation of Romans 8:28: *We know further, that for those who love God, for those called in accordance with his purpose, God makes everything turn out for the best* (SCHONFIELD). We can see why Mother Teresa said that God wants our trust.

> Few of us realize that the secret of happiness is in letting go.[202]
>
> "Let go and let God" – which is so easy to say and for people like me so far from easy to follow…Stop trying to protect, rescue, to judge, to manage the lives around you – your chil-

---

201 Perry Bramlett, Reuben P. Job, Norman Shawchuck, *30 Meditations on the Writings of C.S. Lewis* (Nashville: Abingdon, 2020), 99.
202 Kenneth S. Long, *The Zen Teaching of Jesus*, 75.

dren's lives, the lives of your husband, your wife, your friends — because that is just what you are powerless to do.[203]

What other option is there than to "let go and let God"? So many times in my life, I was foolish enough to believe I could control events and people. Aside from the fact that I had a tough time keeping myself under control, how foolish it was to think I could control others. Acceptance and surrender, after doing all I could and should do, is to allow God to manage the great "whatevers" of life, which are his areas to begin with. If you want to stay upset at least 90% of the time, commit yourself to the management of other people's lives, commit yourself to the management of events with which you are unhappy. Once we stop attempting to protect, rescue, judge, and manage those around us and trust God for whatever, "peace like a river" begins to flow through our lives.

One of my true finds this year was Adam Grant's *Think Again*. The sub-title was what first grabbed me: "The Power of Knowing What You Don't Know." I have already quoted from the book, but now want to give you Grant's two lists for "When You Have It and When You Don't." Although written for the business world, it applies to home, church, and life.[204]

WHEN YOU HAVE IT:

1. See mistakes as opportunities to learn
2. Willing to take risks and fail
3. Speaking your mind in meetings
4. Openly sharing your struggles
5. Trust in your teammates and supervisors
6. Sticking your neck out

---

203 Frederick Buechner, *Listening to Your Life*, 330-331.
204 Adam Grant, *Think Again*, 210.

WHEN YOU DON'T:

1. See mistakes as threats to your career
2. Unwilling to rock the boat
3. Keeping your ideas to yourself
4. Only touting your strengths
5. Fear of your teammates and supervisors
6. Having your head chopped off

QUOTE WORTH THINKING ABOUT

> After thirty years of Parkinson's, I have established a sort of détente with the disease. We have a history together. I've long realized that control is out of the question; instead, I've settled for an understanding that requires adaptability and resilience.[205]

Again, the sub-title of the book was what caught my attention: "An Optimist Considers Mortality." Michael J. Fox has written three books that could have been depressing with the progression of a disease that won't quit. Instead, the books are filled with courage, determination, humor, and lessons on living with a "whatever" nobody would ever want. The keys to his establishing a détente with Parkinson's are spelled out in two words: adaptability and resilience. This involves much more than "going with the flow"; it means creatively and courageously meeting the increasing challenges of debilitation. In one instance, the resilience involved, not eliminating falling, but learning to fall in better ways. One of the questions that will tell us how we are doing with the "whatevers" of life is: how resilient are we? How much ability do we have to bounce back? How determined are we, after failure, to give it another try? Acceptance and surrender need to be paired with adaptability and resilience.

---

205 Michael J. Fox, *No Time Like the Future*, 1.

It takes confident humility to admit that we're a work in progress. It shows that we care more about improving ourselves than proving ourselves.[206]

John Dominic Crossan writes about Jesus' "challenge" parables: "Challenge parables *mean* – that is, intend – to make us probe and question, ponder and wonder, discuss and debate, and, above all else, practice that gift of the human spirit known as thinking. Challenge parables foster not periodic doubting, but permanent questioning."[207]

Recognizing that faith is a "whatever" and involves acceptance and surrender does not mean we simply say, "Oh well," to whatever comes our way. We are meant to be "on the grow" and developing our faith muscles through the exercise of our probing, questioning, wondering, discussing, and thinking. Jesus' parables provide excellent material for all of these. His parables did not so much cause people to say, "Well, that settles that," as it brought a furrowed brow and the thought, "I'll have to think about that a lot more." Almost every parable Jesus tells, in some way, challenges the popular thinking of the day. Responding to the challenge parables as Crossan envisions, will certainly improve the way we handle the "whatevers" that come our way.

COMING TO SOME CONCLUSIONS

Candice Walker became a hero to a patient in a hospital who was writhing in pain on the floor of an elevator. Amazingly, no one seemed to be paying much attention to her, so Candice took charge. She grabbed a wheelchair and took her up in the elevator for immediate treatment. The patient later called her "my savior." What is amazing about this story is that Candice Walker was not a nurse; she was a custodian in the hospital. When she was asked about the incident, she said, "No, it's not a part of my job, but it's part of me."[208]

---

206 Adam Grant, *Think Again*, 210.
207 Peter C. Brown, *Listening for God*, 15.
208 Adam Grant, *Think Again*, 242-243.

The all too obvious lesson is that circumstances (the "whatevers" of life) call for what is in us in order for our responses to be creative and redemptive. We get ready for whatever as we fill our lives with courage, determination, compassion, love, and hope. Becoming the best version of ourselves is preparation for bringing the best to challenging life events. What is in us is what is going to enable us to deal with what is out there. Our biggest mistake is in attempting to fix what is out there and not majoring on what is within us. Michael J. Fox could not "fix" his Parkinson's but he certainly knows how to keep working on himself in order to continue living a productive life.

> Robert Poynton, an innovative thinker about creativity and communication in organizations has come up with: "Everything's an Offer. This foundational principle contains three components: Notice More, Let Go, and Use Everything. Notice more is about heightening our levels of awareness. Letting go is about jettisoning our assumptions, inhibitions and fear of judgment from others. Use Everything means we recognize that everything we note around us, and everything that happens to us, is a potential spark we can use for spontaneous lining and thinking."[209]

Although not specifically a religious book, the advice here of Notice More, Let Go, and Use Everything is a good description of how to enable God to better use whatever happens in our lives for the greater good.

QUESTIONS FOR REFLECTION AND DISCUSSION

1. Do you agree that there is a lot of acceptance and surrender in faith?
2. What do you think about the comment: "The secret of happiness is in letting go?"
3. How did you respond to the two lists of "When you have it" and "When you don't"?

---

209 Roman Krzaric, *Carpe Diem Regained,* 167-168.

Conclusion

Faith Where I Am and How I Am Is The Place for Life and Meaning

I can think of no better summation of all we have discussed than these selections from Deitrich Bonhoeffer's *Letters and Papers from Prison* and Richard Rohr's *The Universal Christ:*

> I discovered late, and I'm still discovering right up to this moment, that it is only by living completely in this world that one learns to have faith…By this worldliness, I mean living unreservedly in life's duties, problems, success and failures, experiences and perplexities. In so doing we throw ourselves completely into the arms of God, taking seriously, not our own sufferings, but those of God in the world – watching with Christ in Gethsemane. That, I think, is faith, that is *metanoia,* and that is how one becomes a man (sic) and a Christian. I'm glad to have been able to learn this, and I know I've been able to do so only along the road that I've travelled. So I'm grateful for the past and present, and content with them.[210]
>
> Spirituality is all about honoring the human journey, loving it, and living it in all its wonder and tragedy.[211]

---

210 Eberhard Bethge, *Costly Grace,* 126-127.
211 Richard Rohr, *The Universal Christ,* 212.

Bibliography Of Quoted Sources

Armstrong, Karen. *St. Paul: The Apostle We Love To Hate.* Boston: New Harvest, 2015.

Aslan, Reza. *Zealot.* New York: Random House, 2013.

Barclay, William. *The Gospel of Matthew,* Vols 1 & 2. Philadelphia: The Westminster Press, 1958.

Beard, Alex. *Natural Born Learners.* London: Weidenfeld & Nicolson, 2018.

Bethge, Eberhard. *Costly Grace.* San Francisco: Harper & Row, 1979.

Blauner, Andrew, ed. *The Peanuts Papers.* New York: Library of America, 2019.

Box, C. J. *Off the Grid.* New York: G. P. Putnam's Sons, 2016.

Bramlett, Perry; Job, Reuben P.; and Shawchuck, Norman. *30 Meditations on the Writings of C. S. Lewis.* Nashville: Abingdon, 2020.

Brown, Dee. *Bury My Heart at Wounded Knee.* New York: Holt, Rinehart & Winston, 1970.

Brown, Peter C. *Listening for God.* Macon: Mercer University Press, 2020.

Buechner, Frederick. *Listening to Your Life.* New York: HarperCollins, 1992.

Carter-Scott, Cherie. *If Life is a Game... These Are the Rules.* Naperville, IL: Simple Truths, 1998.

Cowman, L. B. *Streams in the Desert.* Grand Rapids: Zondervan, 1997.

Dawn, Marva. *In the Beginning, God.* Downers Grove, IL: InterVarsity Press, 2009.

Dodd, Michael. *Thank God for Evolution.* San Francisco: Council Oak Books, 2007.

Duckworth, Angelia. *Grit.* New York: Scribner, 2016.

Evans, Rachel Held. *Inspired.* New York: Nelson Books, 2018.

_____. *Searching for Sunday.* Nashville: Nelson Books, 2015.

_____. *A Year of Biblical Womanhood.* Nashville: Nelson Books, 2012.

The Expositor's Bible, Volume 9. Grand Rapids: Zondervan, 1981.

Flanders, Judith. *A Bed of Scorpions.* New York: Minotaur Books, 2016.

Foster, Thomas. *How to Read Literature Like a Professor.* New York: Harper Perennial, 2014.

Fox, Everett. *The Five Books of Moses.* New York: Shocken Books, 1995.

Fox, Michael J. *No Time Like the Future.* New York: Flatiron Books, 2020.

Francis, Pope. *Happiness in This Life.* New York: Random House, 2017.

Fredriksen, Paula. *Paul: The Pagans' Apostle.* New Haven: Yale University Press, 2017.

Gaillard, Frye. *The Books That Mattered.* Montgomery: NewSouth Books, 2012.

Grant, Adam. *Think Again.* New York: Viking, 2021.

Gregersen, Hal. *Questions Are the Answer.* New York: Harper Business, 2018.

Gregory, Susanna. *The Executioner of St. Paul's.* London: Sphere, 2017.

Guillebeau, Chris. *The Happiness of Pursuit.* New York: Harmony, 2014.

Gurdon, Meghan Cos. *The Enchanted Hour.* London: Piatkus, 2019.

Gutting, Gary. *What Philosophy Can Do.* New York: W. W. Norton, 2015.

Gwande, Atul. *Being Mortal.* New York: Metropolitan Books, 2014.

Harris, Tessa. *Shadow of the Raven.* New York: Kensington Books, 2015.

Hayes, Terry. *I Am Pilgrim.* New York: Emily Bestler Books, 2014.

Interpreter's Dictionary of the Bible, Vol 2. New York: Abingdon Press, 1962.

Johnson, Paul. *Humorists.* New York: HarperCollins, 2010.

_____. *Jesus: A Biography From a Believer.* New York: Viking, 2010.

Kahneman, Daniel. *Thinking, Fast and Slow.* New York: Farrar, Straus and Giroux, 2011.

Kelly, Matthew. *Rediscover the Saints.* North Palm Beach: Blue Sparrow, 2019.

Krznartic, Roman. *Carpe Diem Regained.* London: Unbound, 2017.

Kurtz, Ernest and Ketcham, Katherine. *The Spirituality of Imperfection.* New York: Bantam Books, 1994.

Lenz, Lyn. *God Land.* Bloomington: Indiana University Press, 2019.

Lescroart, John. *The Rule of Law.* New York: Atria Paperback, 2019.

Lidsky, Isaac. *Eyes Wide Open.* New York:: A TarcherPerigee Book, 2017.

Long, Kenneth S. *The Zen Teachings of Jesus.* New York: Crossroad, 2001.

Mankoff, Bob. *How About Never – Is Never Good for You?* New York: Henry Holt, 2014.

Marty, Martin E. *When Faiths Collide.* Maiden, MA: Blackwell Publishing, 2005.

McCullough, David. *You Are Not Special.* New York: ECCO, 2014.

McKenzie, John L. *Dictionary of the Bible.* New York: Macmillan Publishing, Co., 1965.

Merton, Thomas. *Mystics and Zen Masters.* New York: Farrar, Straus and Giroux, 85.

_____. *Passion for Peace,* William H. Shannon, ed., New York: Crossroad, 1996.

Miles, Sara. *Take This Bread.* New York: Ballantine Books, 2017.

Moore, Thomas. *Original Self.* New York: HarperCollins, 2000.

Muggeridge, Malcolm. *Something Beautiful for God.* San Francisco: Harper & Row, 1971.

Murphy, Kate. *You're Not Listening.* New York: Celadon Books, 2019.

The New Interpreter's Bible, Vol VIII. Nashville: Abingdon Press, 1995.

Peters, Thomas C. *The Christian Imagination: G. K. Chesterton on the Arts.* San Francisco: Ignatius Press, 2000.

Platt, Christian. *Post Christian.* New York: Jericho Books, 2014.

Poole, Charles E. *Beyond the Broken Lights.* Macon: Smyth & Helwys, 2000.

Robinson, Marilynne. *Gilead.* London: Vigero Press, 2020.

_____. *The Givenness of Things.* New York: Farrar, Straus and Giroux, 2015.

Rohr, Richard. *Immortal Diamond.* San Francisco: Jossey-Bass, 2013.

_____. *The Universal Christ.* New York: Convergent, 2019.

Ross, Ann B. *Miss Julia Speaks Her Mind.* New York: William Morrow, 1999.

Sayers, Dorothy L. *The Nine Taylors.* London: Hodder & Stoughton, 1968.

_____. *Strong Poison.* New York: Bantam Books, 1985.

Scottoline, Lisa. *Accused.* New York: St. Martin's Press, 2013.

Shelton, Walt. *The Daily Practice of Life.* Rapid City, SD: CrossLink Publishing, 2020.

Shermer, Michael. *Heaven on Earth.* New York: St. Martin's Griffin, 2018.

Shojai, Pedram. *The Art of Stopping.* New York: Rodale, 2017.

Stell, Tom. *A Faith Worth Believing.* New York: HarperSanFrancisco, 2004.

Teresa, Mother. *Come Be My Light,* edited by Brian Kilodiejchuk.. New York: Doubleday, 2007.

Tracy, David. *Filaments.* Chicago: The University of Chicago Press, 2020.

_____. *Fragments.* Chicago: The University of Chicago Press, 2020.

Van Dyke, Michael. Uhrichsville, OH: Barbour Publishing, 2001.

Wilkerson, Isabel. *The Warmth of Other Suns.* New York: Vantage Books, 2011.

Wilkinson, Bruce. *The Prayer of Jabez: Breaking Through to the Blessed Life.* Sisters, OR: Multnomah Publishers, 2000.

Wills, Gary. *What Jesus Meant.* New York: Penguin Books, 2006.

Wilson, Andrew L. *Here I Walk.* Grand Rapids: Brazos Press, 2016.

Wisenthal, Simon. *The Sunflower.* New York: Shocken Books, 1998.

Wright, N. T. *The Case for the Psalms.* New York: HarperOne, 2013.

CPSIA information can be obtained
at www.ICGtesting.com
Printed in the USA
BVHW030916301222
655309BV00002B/305

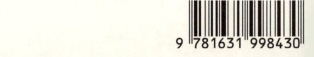